T0146900

Funny Things Happen on the Way to Old Age

Funny Things Happen on the Way to Old Age

Joan Sodaro Waller

Copyright © 2015 by Joan Sodaro Waller.

ISBN:	Softcover	978-1-5035-5853-3
	eBook	978-1-5035-5852-6

All rights reserved. No part of this book may be reproduced or transmitted in any form or by any means, electronic or mechanical, including photocopying, recording, or by any information storage and retrieval system, without permission in writing from the copyright owner.

Any people depicted in stock imagery provided by Thinkstock are models, and such images are being used for illustrative purposes only.
Certain stock imagery © Thinkstock.

Print information available on the last page.

Rev. date: 04/07/2015

To order additional copies of this book, contact:
Xlibris
1-888-795-4274
www.Xlibris.com
Orders@Xlibris.com
540562

Contents

Preface

Why would anyone take the time and trouble to write one's autobiography? I asked myself that question and pondered my answer for some time before I chose this title: *Funny Things Happen on the Way to Old Age.* That did it! I was off and running. What's healthier than recalling funny things about oneself and having a good laugh at your own expense when you are 84 years young?

This characteristic about myself is that "telling on myself" has been a natural attribute of my personality from the "get go." If I goofed, I goofed and everyone heard about it and had a good laugh. As a consequence, I got to be the one to laugh with and laugh at. No problem; that's just the way it was and everyone enjoyed being with me and I enjoyed their "superiority." They kind of took care of me as their "child" in need of assistance.

After Bob and I married and raised three great children, we spent the rest of our life living great distances from our parents, siblings, family and friends. Therefore, those cherished relatives and friends really don't know very much about the "real me" or what I've been up to these many years. Likewise, I know very little about them, the "real them." So, I thought it would be fun to remember on paper how my life was both before and since I knew "them." Then, when I'm gone from this world, at least those who should care about me will at least have something to remember. If not, I hope those who read this book will enjoy the stories and enjoy laughing with me and cheering for me as I tell my tale.

I remember those moments we've shared over the years. Sometimes, I even recall the words you spoke or the activity we shared. Moments which touched and changed me. Thank you for your love, your joy, your words and your deeds. For those who don't know me, I pray you will be informed and entertained. Have a good laugh and perchance you may be inspired to write your own story, funny episodes and all.

May God Bless You One and All!

Chapter 1

GIGGLING GIRLS AND MORE
1930-1948 RIVER FOREST, IL

I was born on October 7, 1930 and I loved my childhood in the 1930s and 1940s.

In spite of the fact that: a widespread depression blanketed the U.S. beginning in October 1929; a dustbowl devastated the Midwest during the early 1930s; and World War II erupted in September 1939 in Europe. When the Japanese bombed Pearl Harbor on December 7, 1941, the United States entered World War II which raged on for years throughout Europe and the Pacific. It finally ended in August 1945 after the US dropped two Atomic Bombs over Japan and peace returned at last.

My friends and I seemed totally unaware of these realities. It's called "childhood innocence," a wonderful state of mind. We giggled through our grade school and high school years seemingly without a care in the world while others suffered extraordinary losses.

Here are a few of our mundane activities:

Hiding in the un-mowed vacant lot and watching to see if our Mafia neighbor's house would be raided by the police that day; planning and executing funerals and burials for our deceased pets; preparing skits and talent shows to entertain our neighborhood, for money of course. We worked on badges for Brownies and Girl Scouts; chased boys and kept our "who am I in love with most" lists up to date. These lists changed at the drop of the hat depending on whether someone looked at, smiled or spoke to us. We played games of Red Rover, Kick the Can, Hide and Seek or we climbed the big oak trees. When we gathered in Annette's father's study and told funny stories, we'd giggle so hard tears ran down our checks. The others went upstairs or outside to play after they stopped laughing and left me alone in the library behind closed doors until I finally got myself under control.

One day, when we were bored, we decided our neighborhood needed a newspaper. We solicited door to door for subscribers to "The Weekly Scoop" and each week we'd searched for bits of gossip or news worthy of print and then set to work. Besides "news," our neighborhood weekly also contained jokes, recipes, stories and poems which we composed. We began publishing our paper by using a gel-based copy pad, but unfortunately, or maybe fortunately, we made such a mess that one of our dad's, a CEO for Sunbeam Corporation, offered to save the situation. He took our hand printed originals and asked his secretary to run off enough copies for all our subscribers. Our newspaper business lasted about a month. Then, we got bored again and searched for something else to occupy our time - something that would take less work and give us more time to play.

"Slumber parties" proved to be a big part of our friendships. Sometimes we would invite up to eight members of the gang for an overnight at one of our homes. I remember on one occasion the "slumbering" or "not so slumbering" gaggle of guests descended on my fourteen-room house. My Mother and my siblings were staying at the farm which left my Dad in charge of me—and my friends. That night there were eight guests who occupied the large living room, equipped with pillows, blankets, games and cards, snacks of many kinds, pajamas, a change of clothes and toiletries. What a mess!

My Father bid us goodnight at a reasonable hour and we continued to party quietly (his bedroom was just above the living room). Some girls finally fell asleep, but when Dad came downstairs in time to go to the office the next morning, much to his surprise, he found several "non-slumbering" guests outside in their PJs greeting the milkman and some still engaged in a game of cards in the breakfast room. We liked having my Dad "in charge" or "not so in charge" as the case may be.

In the winter, the park district created an ice skating rink by flooding a very large circular depression of grass with water. When it froze, we practiced our figure skating tricks from after school until dinner as we dreamed of someday becoming stars in the famous Ice Capades. As darkness fell on the Village of River Forest each evening, we'd return home exhausted and frozen. I'm surprised that over the years I never suffered from frostbite, nor did any of us ever become a star.

Nine months of the year, roller skates and bikes were our modes of transportation. The Village streets and sidewalks were lined with large elm trees which created a canopy of shade overhead. We'd skate and ride all over town with no thought of danger of any kind, except perhaps, skinning our knees by tripping over a raised crack in the sidewalk.

However, during the ragweed season from August 15 until the first freeze, I had trouble keeping up with the group. I carried a tissue box in my bike basket. "Come on, Joan, you're falling behind," they would holler as I constantly stopped to rub my itching eyes and blow my stuffed nose. Usually, they arrived well ahead of me and were already busily engaged in the planned activity by the time I arrived. Roller skating during that season proved impossible for me since there was no place to carry a box of tissues.

Oak Park River Forest High School welcomed me in September 1944 along with 3,000 other eager students. The fall football season opened with my brother, a 3rd string quarterback, sitting on the bench--he, a senior and I, a lowly freshman. I was so proud of Dean, but my friends and I proved to be an embarrassment to him when we hollered, cheered and hooted whenever the coach finally saw fit to put Sodaro in as quarterback anytime our team was headed for an overwhelming victory.

The yellow school bus picked me up at the corner every morning, except on the days when Dean's senior friends invited me to ride to school in Lester's jalopy. I enjoyed sharing the ride with them, especially when we tried to race the school bus by rocking forward as hard as we could to encourage the old car to go faster, but we never managed to win. I hated to ride the school bus. The students were packed in like in a "can of sardines." In the winter, the school bus ride was a nightmare as the overwhelming smell of cigarette smoke saturated our heavy winter coats, scarfs and hats. Since the bus windows remained closed there was no fresh air to kill the odor which was enough to make me gag.

During warm weather we walked home from school through the Main Street shopping district and visited the shops as we went. Eating French pastries at a fine bakery, shopping for clothes and most anything else we thought might be useful. One day at Marshall Field's Department Store I ran into a snag. After I had chosen my purchases and presented them and my charge card to the sales clerk, she left us standing at the counter as she made a phone call. When she returned she said, "I'm sorry Miss Sodaro, but your father has left notice that you are no longer allowed to charge your purchases." Needless to say, I was embarrassed, but I learned a good lesson about not taking advantage of my Dad's generosity.

In anticipation of my forthcoming college expenses, each night my Dad emptied his pocket of every cent of change he'd collected that day and dropped the change into a shoe box or any other container that was nearby. Once he even filled an almost empty glass bath salts bottle. The "almost empty" part became the problem later.

As the first semester of my college career drew near, Dad asked Mom and me to transport the containers of change to the bank. The money was to be deposited in my college fund. Can you imagine how many pounds of change can be collected in approximately 1,500 days or more?

Together, Mom and I carried each box one by one down to the car-and there were many boxes. When we arrived at the bank, one of the officers and a bank guard provided a dolly to bring the boxes of coins inside. Mom was assigned a locked room where she proceeded to hand count and wrap the coins. When I returned several hours later, I too was locked in with Mom and two bank tellers who had joined in her ordeal. It was closing time. The task had become more unpleasant as the bath salts bottle coins got mixed with the clean coins. The room not only smelled like a perfume shop, but the bath salts made everything sticky. It was a mess! The incident of Dr. Sodaro's coins lived on as bank customers and friends enjoyed remembering and retelling the story. By the way, my Father was one of the bank directors and his doctor's office was located right above the bank. I always wondered if he could smell the perfume from the bath salts wafting through the open windows in his office. It was a hot 90-degree day in Forest Park, IL.

P.S. I'm sorry to say that I can't recall how much money was deposited that day and I doubt if anyone is still alive who could tell me. I also am unaware as to whether a coin separator or counter was available at that time in that bank.

Chapter 2

THE RADIO AND ME
1930's 1427 PARK AVENUE, RIVER FOREST, IL

In the 1930s, my memories about the radio usually involve my two brothers, my sister and me. The radio occupied a prominent place at the end of the living room. Couch cushions on the floor provided seating as well as something on which to lie and on which to jump. They were great fun!

My Father's return from his work as a Doctor occasioned the only brief interruption. When he opened the front door and called, "Is anyone at home?" we'd run and give him a hug, check to see if he'd brought us any presents and then rush back to our programs. So much for a warm welcome.

We never wanted to miss a commercial because they were almost as important a part of radio listening as the story itself. I made sure that we sent for the products which were advertised, especially something like the decoder ring which became part of the show.

As I listened, my imagination created the characters and the scenes. What a disappointment it turned out to be when I learned that behind all the sounds I heard and the settings I imagined were simply actors and actresses standing in front of microphones while other people created the sounds of slamming or creaking doors, lightning strikes, thunder boomers, gun shots, horses galloping across the plains, Indians shouting war whoops, someone falling down the stairs and wind whistling through the trees. These actions helped set the mood and brought the stories to life. The actors certainly fooled me, but at least my imagination was stimulated. The stories were as real to me as if I had been watching a movie or seeing the real thing.

We pictured *The Lone Ranger* and Tonto riding across the plains chasing the "bad guys", were terrified by *Inner Sanctum's* creaky door, and wondered what *The Shadow* knew. We laughed at *Jack Benny* and *Rochester's* antics, helped *Dick Tracy* solve crimes, and cried out, "Oh, No, not again," each time everything fell out of *Fibber McGee* and *Molly's* overloaded closet, and cheered *Jack Armstrong*, the all American boy, onto victory, plus countless others.

One day, our Dad brought home a new fancy radio with a remote control box. What magic! Not only could we change programs by rotating the dial from across the room, but now we could even change the stations in our house from the house next door. Why anyone would want to do that I still don't understand, but we enjoyed running back and forth between houses and changing the stations. While one of us took the magic box to the neighbor's house and rotated the channels, the rest of us stared at the radio and listened excitedly as the programs changed from one to another in our house. We'd signal through the window to let the dial changer know that it worked. Then, we changed places and someone else would run next door to be the station changer. That lasted until each of us had our turn. Although this proved to be great fun for a few days, we soon tired of our new "toy" and returned to serious radio listening.

Channel flippers have replaced that remote control box just as the television set in the living room has replaced the radio. Unfortunately, television has deadened the use of our imaginations as "professionals" now supply us with "reality" through the use of their creative imaginations. Consequently, we have both lost and gained. At least we still have novels to read which supply fodder for our imaginations.

Chapter 3

EMBRACED BY LIFE
1930s and 1940s RIVER FOREST, IL

The idyllic, upper middle-class, suburban Village in which I grew up differed remarkably from its neighbors to the north, the south, the east and the west.

On the western border, a half-mile wide strip of dense oak and maple woods hugged the usually quiet Des Plaines River. The woods and the river kept me from an awareness of the industrial town next door while they provided a place where my classmates and I learned first-hand about the birds and bees, the wildflowers and trees. Unfortunately, after several acts of violence were committed in the darkness and privacy of the forest, I grew to fear these woods.

In contrast, on the north, south and east borders of my Village, streams of automobiles and buses belched their sickening gas fumes into the atmosphere; the Continental Baking Company combated the fumes with the sweet-smelling aroma of cream-filled chocolate and vanilla goodies. An elevated train rattled along raised tracks and created a man-made barrier which discouraged interaction with our blue-collar neighbors. Department stores and small shops on the east tempted me with intriguing window displays. Our family's favorite service station overflowed daily with ailing Cadillac's, Chryslers, Packard's and Buicks. My friends and I loved the excitement and enticements of these hustle-bustle-busy borders.

Meanwhile, the interior of my Village wrapped its arms of peace and security around me as I walked, skated and biked about without fear. As a child, I was awed by the stately oak and elm trees which arched their lofty branches across straight streets. They formed a tunnel of shade in the hot humid summer and a maze of snow-laden branches in the cold, blustery winter. My eyes, drawn by manicured lawns, admired the elegant homes nestled shoulder to shoulder beneath them.

English ivy hid the grey stone exterior of my house with its sweeping, shake-shingled roof. It was located in the north central section of the Village surrounded by the noise and laughter of brightly-clad children jumping rope, playing tag and ice skating at the red-brick grade school behind our house, and by giggling blue-uniformed coeds arriving and departing in second-hand jalopies or their parents' cars at the Catholic girls high school down the street. In the summertime, lilacs and roses sent forth their fragrant perfume to delight my senses and oscillating sprinklers called my friends and me to dance in their cool spray. The emerald green lawn often became my family's football field with my brother Dean as quarterback.

Life throbbed within the walls of the fourteen spacious rooms of our house where I lived with my parents, two brothers, two sisters, one grandmother, one maid and a beagle dog named Sugar.

Accompanied by an assorted group of friends, I loved the frenzy of activity that took place within the walls of our home: the thumping sound of jitterbugging feet rose from the basement recreation room while teenage boys lined the slate-floored hall waiting their turn to arrange dates by phone. Younger children fought over game rules in the wallpapered, upstairs bedrooms, the library or the screened porch. Grownups gossiped in the pale-pink living room. Grandma and the maid prepared mouth-watering delicacies in the modern kitchen and we celebrated special occasions in the oak paneled dining room with its leaded glass windows. Sugar weathered the confusion snuggled away in the book-lined library.

At Easter time, the rooms even tolerated the presence of five, fluffy, baby chicks dyed pink, yellow and blue, one chick for each of us. The garage housed a goat who was tethered during the day in the vacant lot next door. All these were gifts from my Father's patients who each year expressed their appreciation by partly paying their bills with animals, homemade delicacies or produce.

In November 1948, I returned to this wonderful home and brought my college roommate home for the Thanksgiving Holiday. I immediately took her around to meet my friends and to invite them to a party at my house. I told everyone to bring their house guests and to tell other friends about the party at 7:00 tomorrow at Sodaro's.

When Janie and I informed my precious Mother that we had invited some friends over for a party on Saturday. I said I wasn't sure how many would come, but we would get some potato chips, dip and soft drinks. On Saturday we set up our party snacks around the basement recreation room. At 7:00 the guests began to gather. About 8:00 I realized the large room was jammed. Some kids were even sitting on the stairs. Worst of all we were totally out of snacks. I took the back staircase to reach the kitchen. "Mom," I blurted out, "I don't know what to do, we're running out of everything."

She put her arm around me, gave me a hug and escorted me into the dining room. The table was laden with a banquet of scrumptious food: every kind of real food which teenagers loved, such as turkey and ham sandwiches, potato salad, coleslaw, pickles, olives, brownies, cookies, etc.

Now I understood why so many kids were sitting on the basement stairs. There was no room anywhere. The house was packed with friends I knew and strangers I'd never seen before. I burst into tears. I'd done it again and my parents had come through once again. Not only was I amazed at the amount of food on the dining room table, but also at the crowd of students who filled the adjacent rooms. You see, eleven months earlier I had made this same miscalculation for the 1947 New Year's Eve party I had hosted. The word had gotten around: "Don't miss a party at Joan Sodaro's house."

I blossomed in this busy home in my quiet Village and in the noise, excitement, allurement and danger which embraced me as I grew into adulthood. The only dark clouds that personally penetrated my carefree, happy childhood were my older brother's call to military service during World War II and my Mother's cancer diagnosis.

When I entered my second year of college, my parents purchased a 120-acre farm with a charming, red-brick colonial house to which I returned for college vacations. I loved the solitude and beauty of country living.

Chapter 4

TWINKIES, SNO BALLS AND
HOSTESS CUPCAKES
1948 RIVER FOREST, IL

It was 1948 and I had just graduated from OPRF High School. My Father informed me that I should get a job for the summer to keep me occupied and to earn some money for college expenses.

So, on a bright, hot, summer morning, I dressed inappropriately in my royal blue, wool suit, stockings and heels to apply for a job. Of course, I also wore the standard pearl choker with earrings to match. It would be my first "real" job interview and I needed to make a good impression.

I started my job search at the Continental Baking Company (Hostess). The Company was located on the north border of my west suburban Chicago neighborhood, River Forest. Since I was dressed so eloquently, it just wouldn't be proper to ride my bicycle. The family's black Packard limousine stood unused in the driveway, so I decided to go off in style.

I must have made a good impression because the manager hired me immediately and said I should report to work at 8:00

the next morning. Wow! I had a job and I would be paid $40 a week. That was easy!

On Tuesday morning, I arrived early and was assigned a locker and received my white uniform. When I put it on over my "good clothes," it felt tight so I took off my suit jacket. The supervisor explained what my responsibilities would be and assigned me to the Sno Ball Division where he taught me how to make Sno Balls.

I followed his brief instructions and was soon busy whipping the marshmallow batter with my right hand and wrist until it became fluffy and light. Then, I took four or more chocolate cupcakes off the rack of trays which stood on my left and placed the cakes topside down on the huge bowl of waiting marshmallow frosting. Now the fun could begin.

With my right hand I dunked the cupcakes one by one under and out of the marshmallow and flipped each one into the bowl filled to the brim with coconut. After I covered the cupcakes with coconut, I placed them on the empty trays which waited on racks to my right.

And so it went: minute after minute, cupcake after cupcake, rack after rack for eight hours. At first, it was fun, but as the hours wore on I was not only exhausted, I was also covered with marshmallow, coconut and cupcake crumbles. That was hard work!

As I left for home, everything I touched felt soft. That is, everything including doorknobs and the steering wheel. Not only were my hands swollen, but so were my feet.

Several weeks later I was assigned a new job. The company was introducing a new product: "Cream-Filled Chocolate Cupcakes" with chocolate frosting and a zig-zag drizzle of white frosting across the top: Behold! "Hostess Cream-Filled Chocolate Cupcakes" were born. As far as I can recall, I was the first employee at that plant to work on the new and experimental product. They were delicious and they became a very popular addition to the Company's offerings.

Here's how they were produced. Once again I stood between two racks of trays, cupcakes to be filled and cupcakes that I had finished filling. This time, however, I had a clever machine to help me produce the new product.

A one and a half-foot wide stainless steel tank stood before me filled with tasty, white whipped cream. On the front, two sets of prongs beckoned me to place the chocolate cupcakes on the prongs two by two. The trick was to know just how much pressure to exert. That was easier said than done. Too much pressure resulted in whipped cream which gushed forth and broken cupcakes which crumbled to the floor. Too little pressure resulted in dry, empty cupcakes which also crumbled to the floor. After many tries and many ruined cupcakes, I finally managed to get the right rhythm and the right pressure. Slowly, hour by hour "Hostess Cream-Filled Chocolate Cupcakes" lined the trays and one by one the racks were wheeled to the frosting station. After the first week I felt like a champion.

Then, came my fall into disgrace. It wasn't really my fault. After all, anyone would be distracted by what was going on at the "Twinkie" belt. It seems that the two women who were "queens" of the "Twinkie" kingdom were in a loud verbal battle over something. Then the physical battle began with them throwing "Twinkies," pulling hair, kicking and screaming. "Twinkies" rolled off the belt onto the floor and the "Twinkie" belt became clogged from all the gooey mess. Finally, the Supervisor rushed in to break up the fight. He tossed the two women out the back door and yelled at the rest of us to get back to work.

I had stood frozen during the excitement and unknowingly had continued to press on the prongs of my little machine. When the fight was over, I found myself bathed in whipped cream which still oozed out of the prongs through the no longer existing cupcakes. I helped clean up my mess and the Boss sent me home to wash. I returned the next day and continued to work until my summer vacation came to an end and college beckoned.

After the first three weeks of work, my Father had inquired, "Joan, what are you doing with the checks you've earned?"

"Oh, I'm putting them in my dresser drawer so I won't spend them." I answered proudly.

"Honey, you can't do that. If you don't cash your checks the company's bookkeeper won't be able to balance their books. Give me your checks and I'll open a savings account in your name." A saving account; that sounded safe to me.

At the end of the summer my Mother and I went shopping for luggage and other items I would need for college. My Father wasn't too keen about the high class, genuine, rawhide luggage we'd picked out, but in spite of the big argument between my parents, I was allowed to keep my purchases. In the end though, I believe Dad was right, though the luggage certainly did last a long time.

My Continental Baking Company adventure into the real world taught me a lot and helped me mature. I even became friends with the "Twinkie Queens."

Chapter 5

OFF TO COLLEGE
1948 SEPTEMBER ST. MARY OF THE WOODS, IN

Going to college in the early nineteen fifties was a far different experience than it is in 2015. Besides one's clothing, bedding, radio and typewriter, one may have added a favorite piece of furniture, a poster board, family photos, a favorite stuffed animal, maybe a boy friend's picture to kiss and, of course, make-up and bathroom items.

The Terre Haute House became the gathering place for new freshman and their parents. The variety of regional accents is what fascinated me most. That first night seemed to be cacophony of voices. At one point I stopped the conversation with my new friends by saying, "You guys sure have funny accents."

I had barely gotten the words out of my mouth when in unison all three protested, "We, have accents? What about you?"

"I don't have an accent," I said in my strong nasal Chicago twang. "In the Midwest we speak the way Americans should speak," I stated emphatically.

"Not so!" replied a voice from Boston, MA, one from Dallas, TX and another from Mobile, AL. That response brought on a laughing jag for all four participants. It became our first lesson in tolerance as we learned to appreciate the regional language and cultural differences we were to share among the students who hailed from all parts of our country and Europe..

St. Mary of the Woods is a small Catholic Women's College located in a wooded farm-land, a half-hour bus ride north of Terre Haute, IN and operated under the auspices of the Sisters of Providence. The campus grounds lay on the edge of a multi-acre farm also owned and operated by the Sisters.

What a contrast to my Oak Park River Forest High School on the west Chicago suburb of Oak Park, IL where 3,000 students were enrolled. St. Mary's enrolled about 200 women only. From day one, I loved everything about being there and still hold fond memories of the Sisters, the students, the classes, the beautiful campus and especially the gorgeous Church.

Since no cars were allowed on campus, when we got bored from lack of social life, occasionally a few girls would hop a train for an innocent weekend visiting friends at Purdue University, Notre Dame University, Indiana University or returned home briefly due to homesickness. I became quite concerned about myself since I didn't feel homesick. To clear up the matter I called home and apologized to my mother. Her reaction really surprised me when she breathed a sigh of relief and said, "Honey, that's wonderful news."

"Why is that wonderful news? I thought it meant that I didn't love you or something like that."

"Oh, no," she said. "Your Dad and I are happy to know how well adjusted you are. That means we did a good job raising you to be independent and self-sufficient. Enjoy each day and have fun. And, of course, study hard, too. We love you!"

I soon learned how much fun a gaggle of girls can have together when there aren't any men around to "fight over or be concerned about pleasing." Life was much less complicated and for me the three semesters at St. Mary's gave me time grow in love with my Catholic Faith and to mature as an adult. But, time moves on and so did I.

****

Before I leave this chapter, let me tell you of a few funny things that happened during my three semesters at St. Mary's which I remember with fondness.

I didn't take a stuffed animal to college like most of my classmate did. Instead, I brought my beloved baby doll whose brand name was Genius so that's what I called her and still do. In fact, she's here right now watching me as I type.

Anyway, one morning as I was getting out of bed I pressed down on Genius' chest and off popped her head. "Oh, my, what shall I do? It's too late to mess with this problem if I'm going to be to class on time," I reasoned.

After I made my bed, I sat Genius' body one my bed where it belonged, put her head on my dresser and went about my daily activities and soon forgot about my injured friend. When I returned hours later, a note, addressed to me lay on my bed. It read, "Joan, see me at once! Sister Georgiana"

"Oh, oh. What in the world could I have done?" I asked myself as I hurried down the hall and knocked on Sister's door.

"Hi, Sister, you wanted to see me?"

"Yes," she said. "I wanted to know what kind of a mother would decapitate her child and then blatantly leave the child headless and run off?"

"What?" I answered puzzled, having forgotten all about Genius.

"Well," Sister said with a slight smirk on her face. "I went into say Good Morning to Genius and I found her in great straights and her mother nowhere in sight. I was shocked!"

Then she burst into the biggest, heartiest laugh and gave me a warm and loving hug. I loved that Sister and I knew she loved me enough to tease me about such a funny circumstance. She was as attached to Genius as I was.

She was also the Sister I went to see in order to solve a mystery. Rumor was rampant about who the Sisters had chosen to pray for to receive a vocation to the religious life. So I asked straight out, "Sister, are you praying for me to enter the Convent?"

"No, not you. You stay in the world and spread your boundless joy," Sister replied.

"Oh, okay," I responded and breathed easier. After that I no longer concerned myself about the matter. "They're probably praying for some of the "not such hot shot girls," I reasoned. Well, it turned out that the two of the most outstanding, popular and "with it" freshman were the ones who actually entered the Convent the following year. That was an eye opener. So much for my insight into God's opinions about people and choices.

****

When I moved into the upper class dorm my sophomore year, each morning I descended the staircase which passed by the College President's Office. Every morning I waved as I greeted Mother Eugenia. After almost two weeks of this kind of encounter, Mother invited me into her office. PANIC!

"Please sit down, Joan. I want to get to learn more about you," she said.

"What would you like to know, Mother?" I asked hesitantly.

"Well, I understand that you have four brothers and sisters."

"Yes, that's right, Mother" I agreed.

"Well, dear don't you think it a bit outrageous that you'd ask your parents to buy you thirteen pairs of eyeglasses with all the expenses they have raising a family of five children?" she reprimanded me.

"Oh, but Mother, I only have one pair of glasses."

"Then why do I see you every day with a different pair?" she puzzled.

"Well, Mother, I actually have only one pair of frames, but I have thirteen different colored insets to clip into that frame so each day I change the insets to match my clothes."

"Oh, praise be to God! I was beginning to think you were the most spoiled student in this school. What a relief! You may go now and thank you for the explanation. God bless you, my child."

"Whew! I dodged another bullet!"

****

As you might expect, there was no smoking allowed anywhere on campus except on the tennis courts or in the lodge on the edge of the property. Since I didn't smoke, it meant I would miss out on all the fun chatting with my friends when they gathered to smoke. Either I would have to join them and put up with the sickening smoke, or, being the friendly type, I could choose to join them and be a miserable. Then one day, somebody suggested that, if my two other non-smoking friends and I smoked, we wouldn't even notice the smell. So, the next time we took the bus to town, we pooled our money and bought a carton of cigarettes to share. That meant that each of us were allowed one cigarette a day so we could join the others once a day in the lodge or on the tennis courts and not miss out on the chatter. It worked! When I returned home for Thanksgiving my friends asked, "Joanie, have you started smoking?"

They were surprised when I said, "Yes."

They asked me, "How much?"

When I told them "one a day," they were shocked.

"You smoke one pack of cigarettes a day????"

"Oh, no. I smoke one cigarette a day," I said and explained the situation. Now, they were totally dumbfounded. You see, my friends at home had been smoking heavily for some time. I had been the only hold out.

However, when I transferred to Lake Forest College in 1950 there was nowhere on that campus where students didn't smoke. I fought a losing battle and I lost.

Chapter 6

IT ALL STARTED ON THE
DORMITORY DRIVEWAY
1950 LAKE FOREST, IL

January 1950: As my brother backed the car down the driveway of Saint Mary of the Woods Le Fer Hall loaded with my possessions, Paula came running after the car waving frantically.

"Joan, I just remembered who I know at Lake Forest College. His name is Bob Waller. I went to high school with him. He's a great guy. Look him up."

"Okay, will do," I shouted back as my older brother, Dean, drove away from Saint Mary of the Woods College after a wonderful eighteen months enjoying female companionship. I was now off to new adventures where the guys were.

February 1950: At my first Lake Forest College "February HOP," I waved to Jean and her date across the dance floor. They looked like a "couple of fuddy-duddys." As we danced by she introduced me to her date.

That night in the dorm: I said to Mary, "Tell your date that I could teach him how to dance."

Phone call the next night: "Hi, Joan, I met you at the dance last night. Mary told me today that you want to teach me how to dance. Would you like to start my lessons at the dance this Saturday?"

"Well, I guess that would be okay. What did you say you're name is."

"Bob Waller," he responded.

"Oh, now I remember."

Then he pressed on. "Why not go to a movie Friday night so we can get acquainted?"

"Okay, I'll be ready at six- thirty."

Thanks," he said and I imagined him smiling at the other end of the line.

Saturday night & dance lesson #1: As soon as the music started, my partner pulled me in real close. Wow, was I surprised! We waddled and rocked back and forth, more or less to the music. Then Jean and her new date passed us by looking like a "couple of old fuddy duddys," dancing a "mile apart." Lesson #1 was completed, without my instructions. So it was Jean who had a "problem."

Sunday and a wonderful surprise:

"Would you like me to pick you up for church in the morning?" he asked

"Sure, that would be fine, but I go to the Catholic Church for 9:00 a.m. Mass," I explained.

"That's no problem. I'll come over about 8:45," he said as he waved and smiled as he headed for his dorm.

When it was Communion time I went forward to receive the Sacred Host; Bob followed me up the aisle and received also.

"I'd better explain the facts to him," I promised myself. So when we exited the church I blurted out, "You shouldn't have done that!"

"Done what?" he puzzled.

"Protestants aren't allowed to receive Communion in the Catholic Church."

"I am Catholic," he proclaimed.

"You can't be Catholic and be in charge of religious activities at a Presbyterian College," I said emphatically. My logic was seemingly infallible.

Then he informed me of the facts. I must say that I was absolutely delighted that I had been wrong. What a wonderful surprise. He was Catholic.

Continuation: We continued to rock and waddle back and forth together on the dance floor through the next 50 years, but when the beat of the music turned on my rhythm button, Bob would hold my hand so I could cut loose and rock and roll by myself. In 2000, we moved to The Villages and enrolled in ballroom dance classes. Though we're still amateurs, at least we've moved away from rocking and waddling back and forth. Now, after a couple of drinks and wearing slippery-soled shoes, we can do a few spins, a walk through or two, perform dips, and no longer is fast-beat jitterbug music a problem for Bob. We'll continue to work on improving those few steps if my clicking knee doesn't get locked and Bob's touch of arthritis doesn't get worse.

EPILOGUE:

And to think it all started on a driveway when Paula shouted to me: "Look up Bob Waller. He's a great guy."

On our movie date, when Bob mentioned he was from Mendota, IL, I recalled

Our romance may have come about in a kind of backwards way, but we have managed to "dance" together through sixty-four years of an interesting, challenging, wonderful and productive life and we're still going strong.

Paula was right. Bob Waller is a great guy and he admits that I'm not too bad either. And guess what?

Now, I CAN EVEN REMEMBER HIS NAME. IT'S MINE TOO!

A STAR IS BORN?

During the Spring Semester LFC puts on an annual variety show featuring students. Bert and I were selected to do a song and dance number to "I Have a Lovely Bunch of Coconuts." We sang with a Cockney accent and danced with gusto as we mimicked a Brit selling coconuts at a local fair. Our rendition was chosen as one of the acts to be performed for the annual Alumni Association Meeting at the Furniture Mart in Chicago during Spring break.

That was all well and good except for the fact that having recently arrived on campus: #1 I didn't know what an Alumni Association was or who would be present; #2 I didn't really know who else would be going; #3 I wasn't familiar with the location of the Furniture Mart or even what it was; #4 My parents had moved to the country about thirty miles west of downtown Chicago and I was unfamiliar with the highways; and #5 I had to drive there in the family limousine alone at night.

I managed to arrive at my destination on time and to find Bert. We performed our act, said goodbye and left separately. I found my car and drove home safely, but in a daze. My parents had waited up for me and asked me all the usual questions.

"Did your act go well? Did the audience clap enthusiastically?"

"I don't know," I answered still in a daze. "I remember nothing about the evening except that I did something for some people I didn't know and I have arrived home safely." My parents worried about my state of mind.

When I returned to school a week later and said to Bert, "We must not have done our act very well since no one clapped when we finished," he flipped out.

"What do you mean, 'no one clapped?' We had two encores and a standing ovation. You were great! They loved us!" he exclaimed.

I called my parents right away to tell them what had really happened. Needless to say, they were relieved and so was I.

The next four semesters were filled with excitement, challenges, successes and lots of fun and growth. I just wish I could remember clearly being a star for that moment at the Furniture Mart in Chicago. Oh, well, I do remember clearly other special moments during my junior and senior years which I still cherish such as:

Participating in our sorority's homecoming float: "Augies Gone To Pot" which consisted of a tropical island float complete with a lion, girls in leopard skin garb, palm trees and a large black pot in which to roast a player from the opposing team, Augustana College. I was chosen to be "Augie" who was roasted in the pot while the leopard skin clad natives poked and prodded me. It was a hoot! We won first prize.

Reestablishing a local sorority, Sigma Tau, and processing it into the national sorority, Alpha Phi.

Getting "pinned" while Bob's fraternity serenaded us with their special song "Delta Chi Sweetheart, I Love You" as he attached his fraternity pin to my dress. It was December 6, 1951. We were engaged the following Spring and married in August 1952.

Chapter 7

RESPONSE TO AN ENGAGEMENT PROPOSAL
1952 Winter LAKE FOREST, IL

Dear Sir:

In regards to the matter which we discussed Wednesday, April 4th, 1951 concerning a certain article of metallic quality, I have reconsidered your offer. I find that after reiterating the advantages and disadvantages of your offer, the weight of the advantages or should I say the good aspects of such a proposal have changed my decision.

If you still think such an offer on your part is feasible and you still feel the same about your proposal, I believe there is a definite market and that the matter might work out for both parties concerned. However, if you have reconsidered and find that at this time you are dubious about the original plan, your client "will go along" with your final decision.

I find that my plans are such that it would be possible to see you this evening in order to complete our negotiations.

Thank you for your thoughtful consideration and patience.

Most Sincerely Yours,   Joan Sodaro   p.s. I love you!

Chapter 8

SADNESS APROACHES
1953 A LETTER MEDINAH, IL

Dear Mary Ann* and Bill,   November 18, 1953

I assumed the other day when the phone call came thru from California that it must be you. It has been a good thing that your Aunt did the letter writing for the family for I am one of the worst. Now that I do have [time] to write myself it isn't so good.

Of course, as you know this has been coming on for a long time and the day has to come sooner or later. It has been seven years since the breast operation and I believe God has been very kind to us to be able to go on as long as we have. The love involvement has been well subdued, but the liver is involved as well as the bowels. There isn't but very little pain to all of this. Most of the time she is mad because she doesn't feel up to snuff. You know her, "on the beam Maggie." It is now getting to the point where her bowels don't move and she doesn't hold food very well.

I don't know how she can go on more than 7 to 10 days. I am staying home to take care of her because hospital care is a cold proposition. I can do so much more for Mom here.

As for your coming here, it doesn't make sense, even though I am sure Mom wouldn't want anything better. There is no cure for her and nothing anyone does is of anything but moral support and that sure doesn't go very far. You have your hands full with your family and that's what you should do. I'm sure that Mom would agree with this if I would ask her, which I am not going to do of course.

Joan's Bob went into the service yesterday. Don came home for a week or longer. Janet is up at school waiting every minute for a phone call. The kids all know what's going on except Peggy. I haven't told her yet because I don't believe she will fully understand until things happen. They sure are all good sports though and feel this very deeply.

Mom and I sure would have loved to have made the trip west as we had planned, but it just was not to be, I guess. She sure would have loved to see your kids and you and Bill and of course me too.

Take good care of your family. I will write you again or wire you just to let you know what is going on.

Our love to all of you,   Uncle Joe [my Dad]

Note: My Mother died November 20, 1953
*My Cousin

Chapter 9

TIDAL WAVE # ONE
1957-1981 CHAMPAIGN, URBANA, & ST. JOSEPH, IL

As Bob pursued his graduate school work, I was briefly employed as a file clerk, a nursery school worker, took in ironing and did child sitting. Later, while raising three wonderful children: I worked part time as a 4th grade teacher's aide; taught kindergarten briefly; served as a data entry person; and volunteered at the Clothing Center at Hays School.

BEGINS IN 1958 ST. PATRICK'S PARISH

The real tidal wave began innocently enough when a friend asked me to be a St. Patrick Parish "BAND LEADER" for our neighborhood. That didn't sound like a big deal, so of course, I said, "Sure"- an answer which, little by little, engulfed, blessed and changed my life. Since school and the park programs were the center of the children's lives and Bob's work towards his graduate degrees, teaching at Urbana High School and finally teaching at the University of Illinois were foremost on his mind, I let the tidal wave overtake me.

Teaching 8th grade catechism for a couple years perked my interest in learning more about my Faith. Then joining the Altar and Rosary Society and saying "yes" to becoming chairman of the LIBRARY AND LITERATURE COMMITTEE enhanced that desire.

As I eagerly read all the pamphlets I ordered, a hunger began to grow in me for more and more knowledge and understanding of the Catholic Faith into which I had been baptized at birth. I soon graduated from pamphlets to books and then to scholarly lectures sponsored by the Newman Center at the University of Illinois in Champaign. The more I learned, the more I wanted to learn. It also led me into a deeper involvement in St. Patrick's Parish life.

Nine months later, the President of the ALTAR & ROSARY SOCIETY instructed me in the ways of the Society and turned the President's gavel over to this eager, young, energetic newcomer. I gathered up other young women my age and for two years we were engulfed in everything from cleaning, painting and curtaining the Rectory basement where we met; to establishing a nursery room; reorganizing the parish neighborhood bands; and of course, setting up chairs and tables countless times for meetings and other events that used that space and sponsoring the Cellar to Garrett Sale fund raiser. The Associate Pastor forbid me to cut any more mimeograph stencils or to run them off on the mimeograph machine because the old typewriter I used cut holes out of the zeros and letters like o, a, e, p, d, etc. This caused the ink to run through the holes making a mess of the machine. That "job loss" proved a blessing for me because many more exciting activities began to occupy my life.

First, in order to help care for our needy parishioners we established THE ANNETTES HELPING HANDS ORGANIZATION. Our first client was a friend who had seven children and was suffering from terminal cancer. Her husband and their children were extremely grateful for our "helping hands" during this crisis in their lives. The most difficult part of this ministry was facing the reality of our own mortality as we watched a friend struggle to live. Francis proved to be an incredible witness to the Grace of God as we watched her grow more courageous, loving and self-sacrificing as the weeks passed. What a privilege to have served our friend and her family. Other cases followed.

One Sunday, the Associate Pastor of St. Patrick's asked if someone would befriend and help an elderly parishioner who was handicapped and alone. The plea touched my heart so I told Father I would find someone to help. "I'm sorry, Joan, but I just can't take on anymore projects right now." Time after time in the back of my "head" I kept hearing, "How about you, Joan?" A week later after many refusals, I understood God's message, so I promised Father that I would be glad to look after Katherine. Thus began several years of commitment to not only Katherine, but also to my neighbor, Lucy. Strong friendships developed and each of our lives changed because of these relationships. To serve these precious eighty/ninety year old suffering servants and later other needy souls, was an honor. I'm so glad I listened to the call of that voice saying, "How about you, Joan."

The Second Vatican Council ended with directives to each parish around the world to implement LITURGICAL REFORMS. Our Siena Study Group encouraged and supported our Pastor as he endeavored to make these reforms such as turning the altar so the priest faced the congregation and other changes. These changes proved difficult for many parishioners and clergy to accept, but through study of the Vatican II documents we gained a better appreciation for the reason for the changes. Eventually, most parishioners managed to move forward.

The more I worked with the Parish the more I saw the need for a PARISH COUNCIL. So, I drew up a plan and presented it to Father. He looked it over and agreed to consult other leaders. As a result, St. Patrick Church may have been the first parish in the diocese to have a lay council to assist the Pastor.

Our first PICTORIAL DIRECTORY and a booklet which described each parish activity were published. This helped parishioners become better acquainted and more involved. Both endeavors entailed countless hours of organizing, but in the end they proved invaluable.

After the church was remodeled and much of the religious art had been removed, DECORATIVE BANNERS were needed to enhance the new, up-dated post Vatican II stripped-down decor. Even though my co-worker and I were neither artists nor seamstresses, we did manage to produce some twenty five "works of art," - some of which were dramatic while others were inspiring and thought provoking.

As our parish SIENA STUDY CLUB members studied the social problems of the times, we were eager to join in finding solutions to local problems in the Champaign-Urbana community. We joined other Christian churches and had our parishioners sign an OPEN HOUSING COVENANT which discouraged white families from fleeing as black families began to move into white neighborhoods. This "stand firm campaign" helped to bring about integration slowly and without violence.

Working through the University's INTERNATIONAL STUDENT OFFICE we provided hospitality to our foreign students by hosting social functions to encourage parishioners and students to become familiar with each other's cultures. Some families even "adopted" students during their duration of study at the University of Illinois.

We hosted students from Egypt, Pakistan, China, Japan, India, Columbia, the Philippines and Russia from whom our children learned to appreciate other cultures. I especially remember the Sunday when our Indian students prepared one of their traditional meals in our kitchen. Cooking food in an open skillet full of hot oil meant the stove and surrounding area became saturated with oil, but the food was delicious and their kindness was appreciated.

During the ecumenical movement, our parish joined CHURCH WOMEN UNITED, a Protestant organization dedicated to ecumenism. We were the first Catholic parish to be involved and I had the privilege of serving as St. Patrick's representative.

The tidal wave of activities continued into the mid 70's. As the abortion issue became more radicalized, our concern grew into action. Once again "Yes" was the answer and a group of Pro-Life supporters bonded together to start a BIRTHRIGHT CHAPTER to help pregnant women who were dealing with this decision. Before we opened an office, we took calls at home so each time the phone rang when I was on duty my heart skipped a beat. Would this call be from a woman in crisis or a friend calling about some mundane matter? Eventually, an office was established downtown where we manned our hot-line 24/7 and where women could drop by for information or just to talk.

It was both heartbreaking and heartwarming to be a phone listener or sometimes to meet with a troubled woman who faced an unexpected pregnancy. I remember on one occasion, walking the streets as snow fell, listening as "Becky" poured out her heart. We walked and talked as she worked through her options. When babies were saved and lives were redirected, we rejoiced, but we were saddened when baby's lives were sacrificed. That night Becky chose life!

Next, a group concerned with hungry, homeless people who lived on the streets of our communities, rented a large house and began to provide delicious, nutritious soup and bread for the "street people." The CATHOLIC WORKER HOUSE also provided overnight housing for women and children. The meals and sleeping accommodations which were provided for those who came to the house enriched the lives of both the workers and the visitors with opportunities to understand one another and to learn compassion.

One day it was my turn to open the house for the lunch guests. I was there alone. The others were to arrive in twenty minutes. All of a sudden, I heard loud banging on the front door and saw a wild looking client shouting obscenities, cursing and arguing violently with someone I couldn't see. I was terrified and hid so he couldn't see me through the window. Needless to say, I prayed for courage and wisdom. Fifteen minutes later, a car pulled into the drive and I could hear a friendly male voice speaking to the deranged man. It took the worker some time to convince the man to move along. He was reminded of the rule about no drinking and no weapons being allowed if someone wanted to come to the HOUSE to eat. After the man had calmed down, I realized he was one of our regular visitors. On the days he was sober, he was a most enjoyable guest, but when drunk it was a different story. That was the first time I experienced the wrong side of this poor afflicted soul, but the next time I served him we had a pleasant time visiting over a bowl of soup. In his past life he had been a nuclear physicist.

These projects made my life meaningful and I loved the people with whom I was blessed to share my time, but when our kids returned home after school, I enjoyed caring and sharing my life with them equally as much.

Chapter 10

REAL CHRISTMAS JOY
DECEMBER 1958 CHAMPAIGN-URBANA *NEWS GAZETTE*

"It will be a sacred and joyous Christmas for the Robert A. Waller family of 1302 Briarcliff, Urbana, IL.

In a letter to the *News-Gazette*, the Waller family expressed the real spirit of Christmas so well, we want to share it with you.

It is the *News-Gazette's* Christmas wish that the Waller's Christmas time peace and joy is typical of every family in Champaign-Urbana and East Central Illinois."

****

Dear Editor and Staff of the *News-Gazette*:

We have been more than delighted with your effort to encourage people to "Put Christ Back in Christmas."

We feel our Christmas really begins at Thanksgiving time when requests come from our church and my sorority, Alpha Phi to donate clothes for the poor and to send toys to the children recovering from heart disease at Herrick House.

The second step in the cycle of giving was Bob's traditional party and informal discussion of college life for all his high school seniors who plan to continue their education. Next was the creation of our Christmas card and poem relating our family news and wishing our friends a "Very Merry Christmas and a Blessed New Year."

The days flew by rapidly as we busied ourselves with making and buying gifts, decorating our house, baking cookies, wrapping presents and making all the usual preparations for the event of Christmas.

Our daughter, Peggy Ann, 4, has been her Mommy's big helper. Tommy, 21 months, although too young to help, has lent encouragement by exclaiming joyously at each new endeavor.

Now the sacred day is almost here and the most important preparation is beginning to take shape - the creation of a crib for the Christ Child.

On Christmas Eve, after singing Christmas carols with our neighbors, putting our starry-eyed angels to bed and laying out their gifts, we shall place in the awaiting crib our image of the Baby Jesus.

Upon arising Christmas morning and greeting the Christ Child, our family will attend Mass together in the true spirit of Christmas. Then the opening of gifts, the preparing of dinner and the climax of all, the birthday cake for the Infant Savior and the singing of "Happy Birthday" which the children have been rehearsing daily.

We feel this will be our merriest Christmas ever. For in each act we have performed we have remembered to keep the real meaning foremost in our minds and hearts.

Our wish for this and each passing year shall be - that every family everywhere "Put Christ Back in Christmas" and in return enjoy the blessing that He will shower upon them.

"PEACE ON EARTH TO MEN OF GOOD WILL"

Mr. and Mrs. Robert A. Waller and Family

Chapter 11

TENTS, TRAILERS AND TREKING
1962-1994

In the summer of 1962, a trip to Washington, DC was required for Bob to initiate research for his doctoral dissertation. We decided to make it a vacation for the whole family. What an exciting adventure, but how could we afford to do it?

Our neighbors came up with a brilliant solution to our dilemma. They offered to lend us their tent and everything else we would need to set up camp, including their homemade trailer to carry all the gear. Such a generous gift was hard to refuse so we graciously accepted.

Since we'd never set up a tent before, we decided to practice in our back yard. The workers consisted of Bob and myself, Peggy age nine, Tom age six, and Jim age four. The tent consisted of ten two-piece adjustable poles, multiple stakes to anchor the tent and ropes to support the sides and the roof. We staked the tent bottom to the ground, assembled the poles, inserted them in the various grommets and looped the ropes over the poles.

Next came the raising of the poles and staking them with ropes making sure each pole would remain standing while all the other poles were raised. For this we needed more help.

The additional help which came in the form of sixteen neighborhood children ages four-ten; not the most skillful or reliable workers. In spite of all the capable (?) help, the ordeal lasted three hours of failure and frustration, but at last the tent was standing upright. The workers cheered and we celebrated with a Kool Ade and cookie party. Afterwards, we dismantled the tent and packed all the parts in their respective bags. Bob and I loaded all our gear onto the trailer and placed the tent and its parts on top of the load. Now the question remained: could we repeat the set up without all those additional hands when we stopped at night in Ohio, West Virginia and Washington?

That first night we managed to get the tent set up after much trial and error, but when we unloaded the rest of the gear we found that while we were driving, the cooler had dripped water on the sleeping bags. When the sun set, the temperature dropped into the 60s, so sleeping in wet sleeping bags meant misery and very little sleep.

The second night in the mountains of West Virginia we camped in a violent thunderstorm. What a frightening experience that turned out to be. The tent endured in spite of the storm and the unprofessional way it had been erected; another night without sleep. When we broke camp everything was saturated and covered with mud.

At least when we arrived and established camp in Washington, DC, the weather was dry and hot, a welcome relief for the time being. The next day the tent and our gear had dried out at last. Now the problem was sand, dust and humidity. The campground was located behind the Jefferson Memorial between two rivers. This sounded ideal, but you cannot imagine the challenges this location presented. Since the campground was extremely popular, grass was practically non-existent. Boats glided up and down the rivers blowing their whistles, jet planes from the airport whined overhead, cars streamed passed with horns honking, emergency vehicle sirens wailed in the distance, and campers talked and laughed as children cried and fought. Where was the peaceful silence we had expected? And what about beautiful trees to shade us during the hot, humid days. This was city camping! What else could you expect to experience from an inexpensive government campground located in an area which was convenient to tourist attractions? We did manage to survive in spite of it all.

Some days Bob would drive himself into the city to do research leaving us behind in the hot, humid, dusty campsite. On other days we'd drop him off at the Library of Congress and/or the National Archives while the children and I spent the day sightseeing. To keep busy proved to be a challenge in spite of the numerous sites to visit. At 4:00 we'd pick up Bob and fight traffic on our way back to the campground.

One day we visited the Mint. We couldn't wait to watch money being created, but the hot, humid air and the crushing crowd caused me to become claustrophobic. In my panic, I grabbed the bewildered children's hands, dragged them through the crowd and ran for the exit.

"Mommy stop, I can't see them making the money. Where are we going, please stop! I can't run so fast," they shouted as we pressed forward bucking the crowd. I knew I'd die if we didn't escape. Once the exit door opened and I felt a breath of fresh air float by, I was relieved and soon recovered. Tom, Jim and Peggy just stood by crying and bewildered as I gasped for air. Unfortunately, because of that episode, none of us has ever seen how money is minted.

The next day we headed for the wax museum. I had studied the travel guide and knew exactly how to get there. I had counted the blocks on the map so I knew how far we had to go. As we walked further and further, I realized that all the blocks marked on the map were only the major cross streets. Countless other blocks actually existed in reality. The scenic area I expected to pass through turned out to be an area of DC that had been destroyed by the race riots and violence in the recent past. It would have been scary walking through this district any time, but at this time in history walking with the children through this neighborhood definitely was the wrong place. Although we were very frightened, we had to continue. At last we arrived at the fascinating museum and the children enjoyed the visit. In order to not repeat our last experience, a pleasant and helpful guide gave us different directions, which included a bus ride through a very nice district and twenty minutes later we arrived safely back at our car. Had I known better, I would have driven to the Wax Museum.

Bob's research had gone very well all week as he enjoyed the air-conditioned facilities he used. The children and I suffered, but at least we became somewhat seasoned tourists and had learned something about maneuvering about as visitors. On the return trip back to Illinois, we opted to stay in a motel. Eventually, we bought our own tent and equipment and experienced such things as: a monster turtle sleeping under the tent floor; a tornado; a son's asthma attack involving a four-hour emergency run home to the hospital; an attack by a very large woodpecker; steak stealing raccoons; an escaped convict warning and a bloody accident victim coming of the woods yelling at us. Thinking he was the escaped convict, I yelled, "Go fast!" and then I felt guilty leaving the man behind. In spite of the misery of inconveniences and these occasional scares, we kept camping. Later we graduated to a rented pop-up camper for a trip to Michigan with the children.

After the children were grown, Bob and I purchased a tag along trailer with a full kitchen, bathroom and two spots for sleeping. It cost $3,000 second hand and, as usual, we made improvements. [The next day a friend told us he learned that the salesman had sold the trailer for $1,000 under the actual asking price of $4,000. His boss let it go with the comment, "We'll earn that amount back in repairs."]

The trailer was christened "Little House." We dragged "Little House" behind our van for 45,000 miles, north, south, east and west across the United States. We parked "Little House" on the beach, in the mountains, woods, deserts, plains, people's yards, driveways and even on the street. It provided us with a free portable motel room complete with bed, bath, board and an entertainment center complete with TV, radio, cards and game playing as we watched a nightly campfire through our glass jalousie windows or outside under the stars. When at home we parked "Little House" at the end of our driveway under a big tree and the trailer became my counseling office.

On a trip to Sante Fe, NM we hit snow and icy conditions so when we arrived at our destination the park attendant was not too happy to see us. He warned, "Ordinarily the Park wouldn't allow you to enter with such a dirty trailer." We had no clue as to what he was referring until we glanced back at the trailer. There stood a brown monster. "Little House" was not only encased in mud, it was encased in frozen brown mud. The attendant finally decided to allow us to park outside the camp and to use their hose to bring our trailer into a decent state of being. Together, it took us over an hour to chip through the ice and clean off the mud. What a mess! Thank God that never happened again.

Traveling memories mounted as the years of camping progressed, but the most memorable one happened in the Grand Tetons. The Teton Pass, at an altitude of 8,429 feet, brought us across the Rockies from Nevada back into Wyoming. Ascending the mountains on the Nevada side, put great strain on the Chrysler Van as it dragged the fully loaded trailer up the steep grade to the crest. The van itself was already weighed down with four good sized passengers, luggage and additional gear.

The real problem began, however, as we started down the eastern slope toward Jackson Hole, WY. As we descended, Bob was careful not to put stress on the brakes, but the trailer and additional weight in the car forced the van to gain speed rapidly.

Halfway down the mountain the brakes began to smoke. Then I noticed flames shooting from the wheel on my side. Bob couldn't stop the car and was finally forced to exit onto an emergency rest stop on the side of the highway to let the brakes cool. Our passengers were anxious to catch their flight which caused additional fear and tension. Forty-five minutes passed before the brakes finally cooled and we cautiously continued our descent into the valley. We arrived at the Jackson Hole airport just in time, quickly dropped off our passengers with their luggage and headed for an auto repair facility.

The auto mechanic assured us that everything appeared to be OK, so we continued our trip to Green River, CO with our fingers crossed. State Route 191, a two-lane narrow highway which descended through small mountains and hills, was under much needed road repair. Miles later we found ourselves crossing a very strange bit of almost abandoned flat land. What if something happened in this desolate place we wondered as we kept moving south from Pinedale to Farson, a "nothing town," in the middle of nowhere. We traveled ninety plus miles through this unbelievable geography and later learned we had been crossing the salt flats of Wyoming and Wyoming's bad land hills north of Interstate 80. The relief we felt as we exited this barren area really hit us as we re-entered the real world of speed, noise and craziness. Twelve exhausting hours had passed since we departed the quiet cabin in Nevada, but our day's destination was still an hour away. The next morning the Green River auto mechanic sent us on our way home to Florida with his blessing. We chose to travel via interstate highways-no more back roads!

After we moved to Florida, we planned one last trip which called for traveling west on route 10 across country from Florida to California, up the Pacific coast to Washington State and to return home through the Rocky Mountains, across the Midwestern Plains and back to sunny Florida. But, we were so busy having fun in The Villages, we sold "Little House" and never went on that one last adventure. But "Little House" went without us. The couple who bought the trailer from the dealer took the same trip that we had planned, but they went the opposite direction, going north to Washington, down the Pacific Coast Highway and crossing from California to Florida east on route 10. We never heard whether or not our trailer made it all the way. I'd love to hear about their adventure.

On one trip I composed the following thoughts in regard to traveling:

Traveling is a time to dream, a time to be creative, a time to open one's mind to human potential.

Traveling is a time to trust, a time to explore the wonders of the world and the wonders of oneself. Traveling is refreshing, relaxing, renewing.

Chapter 12

SINK, SANK, SUNK AND GLUG GLUG
1970-2000 URBANA, IL

"What in the world does that mean?" Bob asked me.

"That's what we are going to call our four rubber rafts," I explained with a laugh. "Can't you just see the five of us floating down the river or crossing the lake?"

"What lake? What river? We live in the middle of Illinois corn country and there is nary a body of water within miles."

"Don't worry, somewhere we'll find water to enjoy." And we did.

The rafts were fun and challenging. At last, we were able to get away from the shore and make an effort to go somewhere. They were also a great way to get a suntan. I detest having to lay out in sand or grass. The three one-person, small, round rafts, Sink, Sank and Sunk tended to just go in circles while the two person raft, Glug Glug, went forward as long as the two occupants coordinated their paddling strokes. The ideal place for any raft is a stream or a river and we found the perfect stream in Michigan.

Our friends, Betty and Bob, invited us to accompany them down a beautiful, crystal clear, quiet stream near their vacation home. They rented two canoes which they shared with our three children. Bob and I followed along behind in Glug Glug with large white swans floating alongside pecking at our rubber "boat."

It was a glorious, scenic, peaceful trip, just like I had always imagined. We floated downstream for about thirty minutes when suddenly the stream led into a small lake. The canoes raced ahead of us and soon disappeared from sight. Our craft, however, was buffeted by the wind and under the control of the waves which made it barely possible to move forward. Even when we did make progress, we still had no idea where the stream exited the lake. Though we paddled frantically, the raft remained pretty much caught in the middle of the lake. We began to panic as we sat there helpless

Thirty minutes later, Bob and our son, Tom, appeared out of nowhere and paddled towards us as we waved and hollered to let them know we saw them. They tossed us a rope which we hung onto for dear life as they towed us back into the stream where we were safe and able to move forward once again. Fifteen minutes later, the four of us landed safely on a Lake Michigan beach where Peggy, Jim and Betty joyously greeted us.

****

Several years later when driving past a boat dealership, I decided to stop and see if they sold canoes. There, our son, Jim and I discovered a handsome, bright red Old Town canoe with a parquet floor. It was really something to behold. With Bob's permission and with Jim's savings for a down payment, we purchased the canoe and loaded it onto the top of the car. That day, "The Red Baron" became our family's new mode of water transportation. As the years progressed, we discovered Illinois had many rivers and lakes for us to investigate, both nearby and far away.

Sugar Creek near Turkey Run State Park in Indiana was our first big challenge. We learned the basic skills of canoeing in the swimming pool at Crystal Lake Park, in Urbana, Ill. We also learned the rules of boating etiquette and safety. Unfortunately, our first group of fellow canoeists had never learned either the art or the rules before we joined them in an adventure down this beautiful, but somewhat tricky creek. Before we launched our canoes into Sugar Creek, the Ranger issued a host of warnings including one last instruction: "As you approach the final landing, be sure you pull your canoes high up on the bank before disembarking. There's a steep drop off at that point in the creek."

The beer flowed like the creek and by the time we were to enter the water many of our "friends" seemed somewhat unseaworthy. They ignored all the instructions and warnings which the ranger had given us before we launched. Luckily, Bob and I had learned just enough to be of help when troubles began to present themselves. Sugar Creek would flow quite rapidly, then suddenly the water would become still. Then it would surge and begin to turn and to twist.

Five times we risked our own safety as we paddled back upstream to rescue friend's canoes which were stuck on rocks, dry land or caught in a whirlpool because they either had too much to drink, acted crazily, ignored the hazards or lacked the skills.

Then, as we approached the landing at end of our trip, exhausted and upset, none of us remembered the ranger's final warning to beach the canoes high up on the land before disembarking. Instead, one by one the passengers stepped out into the deep water which left the only person on board to struggle alone trying to bring their canoe under control and to land it high on the bank as the creek flowed silently downstream.

Truly this adventure was a nightmare, but for us it became the beginning of many years of joyful experiences canoeing around the country from Maine to Oklahoma.

****

We purchased a home on Lake Hartwell in the college town of Clemson, SC in 1986. At last the Red Baron came to rest on its own lake down the hill behind our house. Another dream had come true for us.

One year later, just outside of Clemson on highway 93, I spotted a blue and white outboard speed boat "for sale." I drove by three times and then parked the car along the road, took a closer look and copied down the phone number. Mustering my arguments and courage, I hurried home to convince Bob of the wisdom of buying this boat with which I had fallen in love. That night we bought this "real" boat and launched into the joy of racing from here to there instead of paddling slowly and silently. I loved the speed, but I never appreciated the sound of the motor which disrupted the God-given serenity of being on the water. The other advantage, however, was the ability to explore the shoreline and discover quiet coves where we could picnic in the shade and swim off the boat.

As all boat owners say: "Boats are the pit into which you pour money." Of course, we also, found that to be true. One day while we were visiting family in California, our friends across the cove noticed our boat slowly sinking. They notified other friends who helped rescue our boat. When we returned home we found all our gear lying under the carport and learned of the rescue. It seems that heavy downpours of rain had fallen for days and flooded our uncovered boat.

A few years later, we fell in love with a silver, blue and white deck boat which our pastor, Father Chuck christened, "Eutrapelia", a Greek word meaning "pleasure." A few years later, we moved off the lake and sold this boat for cash to a man from Florida. He was thrilled and we were relieved of the burden of maintaining a boat.

That night, as I gleefully counted out the $10,000 cash, I happened to glance at our ad in the local paper. There, just below our notice, was an ad for a white and red Stingray inboard runabout. The next day we went over to the owner's beautiful, immaculate garage just to take a look at his also immaculate boat. You guessed right. Luckily, the hitch was still attached to the car so we bought the boat, attached it to our car, dragged it home and parked it in our carport. For three years, we trailered this beautiful runabout from lake to lake in South Carolina. When we moved to Florida, we sold the "like new" boat, which we never named, to the young couple next door. Together the four of us pushed our boat out of our carport, down our driveway, up their driveway and into their garage. We've been boat-less ever since.

I still miss the joy of being out on the water racing from place to place. We are "land locked" once again, but this time in central Florida where oceans and small bodies of water surround us. It may seem funny, but, for some reason, we are never drawn to enjoy any body of water which we encounter in this state.

I still dream of seeing our deck boat, "Eutrapelia," somewhere here in Florida where it has probably been docked since it left us back in South Carolina at the end of the 1990s.

Chapter 13

WORKING FOR GOD EARNS
BLESSINGS NOT CASH
1974 -1977 URBANA, IL

It all began with: 1). The desire to bring people into a fuller Christian life dedicated to Jesus as Lord and submitted to the total working of the Holy Spirit, 2). The desire to form a community where members would exercise the Charismatic Gifts in their ministry along with all the gifts of the Holy Spirit, 3). The desire to share the life of Christ in a deeper way with fellow Christians by living in community rather than by living in isolation from one another.

In June of 1974, Father Joseph Nickerson and Father Sebastian Naslund, OSB obtained permission from Bishop Edward W. O' Rourke of the Diocese of Peoria to open a House of Prayer in Urbana, Il. After pooling their financial resources, the priests bought an apartment building on West Main Street only to discover after signing the lease that the apartments would not be vacated until the following August.

Luckily, next to the apartment house a Baptist church and parsonage were also for sale. Much prayer ensued and by July both properties were added to their mortgage. Still, there wasn't a place to house the men so an additional house was purchased on West Church Street. The women were to reside in the parsonage and the house on Church Street became the men's residence. By August, everyone was housed and the work was in full swing. Although I lived in my own home with my husband and our three children, I worked with the community full time and became totally dedicated to the goals and work of this ministry. At the end of the first fourteen months of operation, a total of nine workers, clergy, religious and laypeople, had dedicated themselves to the mission of THE GOOD SHEPHERD HOUSE OF PRAYER, including myself.

At the outset, it was hoped that the ministry would be wide enough in scope to cover the physical and spiritual needs of those seeking help. However, after three hectic months it became clear that the ministry was to be confined to serving only the spiritual needs of those who were open and searching for a deeper walk with God or who seriously needed to be set free from their present state of spiritual stagnation or desperation.

The Church and the women's residence had been completely redecorated and renovated both inside and out. New sidewalks and fence were added and a productive vegetable garden had been established.

Professional painters, plasterers, electricians and plumbers volunteered their time. Furniture and office machines, kitchen appliances and equipment, food and financial support arrived like gifts from Heaven. The Sister in charge of the kitchen would pray for a specific item and low and behold the item appeared.

A book store and gift shop which contained original works of art by one of the Sisters on staff did a grand business. The SHEPHERD'S CALL Newsletter had grown from 300 subscribers to 2,300. Twenty renewal weekends and retreats had been held and three Teens Encounter Christ weekends had inspired countless teenagers.

Off and on, a total of thirty visitors lived for a few days in the bedrooms of the renovated classrooms in the church and shared in the life of the Good Shepherd House of Prayer. They enjoyed privately directed retreats and private prayer sessions. An uncounted number of visitors stopped by daily to be prayed over by the community. They found that Jesus' power for healing and deliverance is sufficient to meet any problem including alcoholism, drug addiction, nervous breakdowns, depression and more.

Weekend Teaching Conferences were offered monthly by outside speakers for those who were eager to grow in their relationship with Christ and to experience and to learn how to use the Charismatic Gifts. Hundreds of calls and letters which sought prayer for self or loved ones were received and lifted up in prayer daily. Talks, retreats and seminars were given by the members of the House to residents, neighbors and visitors from a far. Hours upon hours were spent in prayer, praise, meditation, Scripture study and spiritual reading.

We celebrated Mass daily and prayer meetings weekly. A Prayer community and Scripture study groups were begun for high school and college students. Birthday celebrations and other festive occasions were enjoyed by local Christians. Thanks to God's grace, growth and change took place in the lives of those who lived in the House, to visitors, to those who worked with them and to those who participated in any of the activities sponsored by the Staff. It was a joyous, challenging, backbreaking and fantastic time of love and growth. We shared in the work, the fun, and the blessings as we labored together and supported one another along the way.

A life lived by faith in the promise of Jesus that "God would supply all our needs" proved true. I was blessed to be a member of the staff and thoroughly enjoyed my main job as writer and editor of the monthly newsletter, THE SHEPHERDS CALL.

Those who received and read the articles and essays reported by letter or in person how they had found the teachings truly inspiring.

Eventually, the Good Shepherd House of Prayer was moved to Peoria, IL and for a time continued the work begun in Urbana. Working gratis for God earned me a ton of blessings for which I will always be grateful and I remember with great fondness each day's adventures of ministering there.

Chapter 14

A UNIQUE GIFT
1975 NOVEMBER URBANA, IL

My father's 80th birthday was coming up fast and no member of the Sodaro side of the family seemed to have any idea how to make it a special day. My father and stepmother lived in the country west of Chicago and wintered in Boca Raton, FL. Dean lived in the west Chicago suburbs, Don resided in California, Janet in Florida, Peggy in Maryland and I lived in central Illinois. Our family members weren't letter writers and phone calls were rare. Although we had grown up together, our lives as children and now as adults were pretty much disconnected.

Our Stepmother turned 75 two years before. Since the majority of the Berliner side of the family lived in the west Chicago suburbs, they were able to physically work together to create a spectacular celebration, writing skits and lyrics which they often practiced together. They presented her with countless gifts and planned a big surprise party for all "Mom's" family, friends and relatives. It was a truly memorable and fun-filled event which this tightly knit family had produced.

Now, the question was: "How could we come up with an equally great gift for the Father we all loved?"

Since I was the oldest daughter, I felt it was up to me to spearhead some action. Calls went out to my brothers and sisters. We talked several times, but no interesting or special suggestions came as a result. Time lapsed, October arrived and so did my cousin from California.

Mary Ann is like an older sister to us. She is an enthusiastic, loving person who really appreciated all that my Father had done for her after her mother died. During her short visit we discussed the dilemma daily, but no ideas were generated. She suggested that I call everyone again. As I dialed my older brother's number, suddenly an inspiration popped into my mind. Shocked, I almost dropped the phone. As I explained the inspiration to each sibling, their immediate reaction was wholehearted enthusiasm. "Yes," they agreed, "this is the right solution."

The inspiration for "A BOX OF LOVE" and for "A MAN FULL OF MEMORIES" had been conceived and was about to bear fruit. The overall title would be "SOMETHING DIFFERENT FOR DAD."

What joy, what relief and what fun the next few weeks held as word went out to all the various family members and friends across the country. Even some of my Father's faithful patients became involved. The following weeks were a time of thought provoking memories, soul searching, creative thinking and writing for each of us: a time of love rekindled.

There were two parts to the special gift: sealed love letters from all family members, including the youngest, and many friends and relatives. The second part called for everyone to find pictures of Dad which provoked fond memories of friendship, fun and love. The letters were to be private, addressed to Joe, but sent to me in a separate envelope. The collection of photos would be placed in an album. Birthday wishes by phone were encouraged for later.

The days flew by and the "secret love letters" and photos began to fill up my mailbox. Now, I needed to find a beautiful, hand carved, wooden box to hold the multitude of correspondence and a beautiful album to hold all the photos which family members and friends shared.

Mary Ann's letter and photos arrived first followed by one of my stepsisters. Slowly the letters and photos began to arrive. I was excited about the plan, but as the days passed doubts began to stir. "What if someone didn't like the idea and refused to write the letter? What if Dad was more hurt by the letters that didn't get written and sent than blessed by the ones who did respond? By the time of the shipping date all family members except one had responded. I learned later that they had misunderstood the directions and sent their response directly. It was time now to tie ribbons around each family's letters, glue the last picture in the photo album, box up the two gifts and send them to Dad's winter residence in Boca Raton, Florida in time for the big day.

The picture album entitled "A MAN FULL OF MEMORIES" had eight chapters:

1.) "A Man Named Joe" including Dad as a student, actor, doctor, farmer, father, friend, party person and land developer,
2.) "Dad's two loves," our mother and our stepmother,
3.) "Joe on the go" showing his many automobiles,
4.) "Homes he owned" and
5.) "Activities that caught his fancy" such as: fixing a broken pump; driving a tractor, a snow plow, or a pickup truck full of grandchildren; parties, picnics, weddings and dancing; cheering on the Fighting Illini; building corncribs; traveling and sunning himself in Florida; boating, horseback riding, outdoor barbequing, deep sea fishing and playing his favorite game, golf.

Unfortunately, there were no pictures of the Doctor making house calls; in the hospital delivering babies, healing bodies and saving lives; in the office helping patients or in the Forest Park National Bank serving as an officer. Throughout the album most of the family and many of his friends could be located.

Our Dad is a man who lived a life packed full of service to others, joyous celebrations, creative and constructive projects including: owning and being a gentleman farmer of a 325-acre farm in Big Rock, Illinois, as well as developing Medinah Country Estates, a 120-acre subdivision in Medinah, Illinois.

The fruits of our labor arrived on schedule and the impact on Dad proved to be truly a God-given inspiration. Without my knowing it and like the miracle of the loaves and the fish, the inspiration had multiplied. Not only had all the family members participated, but our Father had also received letters from long ago neighbors, patients, colleagues, friends and other distant relatives. Each morning for days Dad read a few of the letters and studied the pictures with feelings of joy and gratitude for being blessed with a loving family and a life filled with happy memories and many accomplishments.

Later, I learned that the letters came in all shapes and sizes, colors and forms of expression; on notebook or typewriter paper; typed, printed, or in cursive writing; folded carefully or haphazardly; in large and small envelopes, both white and colored; neat and artistic, wordy, articulate or brief; poems, allegories, descriptive phrases and letters were all used to convey the message, "I love you." The wooden box held a true mosaic of our personalities.

So, in spite of distance, time, lack of money and frustrating circumstances, we had truly come together in love and produced "SOMETHING DIFFERENT FOR DAD." It was a birthday surprise that we will never forget.

As frosting on the cake, so to speak, his friends in Florida hosted a delicious dinner party for him. Then, Dad and Mom, the greatest party givers of all, put on a cocktail party for their friends in return.

Chapter 15

FINALLY, A REAL JOB WITH REAL PAY
AN INTERLUDE
1975-1981 CHAMPAIGN-URBANA-ST JOSEPH, IL

As Peg, Tom and Jim entered their college years, I decided to get a real job so I applied to an employment agency. When the interviewer said, "Tell me about yourself." I quickly replied, "I'm a 'NEAT NICK.'" He informed me, "I have just the job for you." That's how I became a teller at the BANK OF ILLINOIS in Champaign, IL and later a teller/bookkeeper at the BANK OF ST JOSEPH, St. Joseph, IL. I hadn't earned a salary for many years so when my first paycheck was handed to me I was surprised. I was having so much fun working I'd forgotten all about being paid.

I felt safe handling all that money until the day when a customer approached my window and handed me his withdrawal slip. I smiled pleasantly, gave him his cash, then as I flipped the slip into my drawer I read the words on the reverse side. "This is a hold-up. Give me all your cash in a bag." My heart stopped. Then, I relaxed as I noticed the gentleman walking out the front door. I plopped down on my chair and breathed a sigh of relief loud enough for the tellers next to me to hear. "What's wrong?" they asked quietly. "Oh, nothing, now. I'll tell you later."

Later on I worked in a kiosk bank drive in where the teller is separated from the main building. My kiosk located in the middle of the drive up meant that each day I had to send my cash drawer underground on a shuttle from the main vault to my station. I walked across the driveway and opened the kiosk with a special key and retrieved my cash drawer from the shuttle. It was very pleasant out there away from all the hustle-bustle. My phone line connected me to others when needed.

I was happy out there and felt safe except for one time. It was late afternoon and as I was busy preparing to close up for the day. When I turned back toward the window and I found myself staring into the face of the most horrible-looking woman with wild eyes and hair sticking up straight. Her face was totally distorted as she pressed it hard against the window. I let out a piercing scream and the woman vanished. Grabbing my purse, I ran quickly to my car, jumped in and locked the door. That night I couldn't sleep both because of the woman, and because I was concerned about my cash drawer which I had left sitting on the underground shuttle instead of locking it back in the main vault. Luckily, the next day my cash drawer was still sitting quietly underground, so I pressed the button and sent it back to my station outside.

I later learned that the poor woman lived on the streets and roamed about town all day. I saw her once again when she wandered into the main branch where she fooled around with the deposit slips and left. She wasn't as horrible-looking in reality as I had experienced her with her face smashed against the window glass.

Another day, while working diligently as a bank teller at the inside drive up window I heard my supervisor say, "Joan, you have a phone call from the hospital, it seems that your son, Jim, has been in an automobile accident and is in the emergency room. Take the call on line three."

I grabbed the phone. "Yes, yes, I understand. How is his car?" I asked calmly. "Oh, that's good. Thanks."

As I headed back to my teller window at the drive up voices were asking, "What happened? Is Jim alright?" What are you doing?" "Aren't you going to see him?" other tellers asked.

"I can't. I'm working," I replied. "I can't leave work. It isn't closing time," I reasoned. The next thing I knew, they handed me my coat, purse and keys and shoved me out the door. I almost felt like a volunteer once again. So there was some freedom even when being paid for what you're doing.

When I reached the emergency room, the attendant pointed to a curtained room where I was surprised to see one of my bank customers waiting for help. "Mrs. Barkly, what happened to you?" I asked shocked.

"Oh," she replied, "some young kid ran into my car."

Just then from behind the curtain next to me I heard, "Hey, Mom, I'm over here!" says Jim. At that I made my apologies, wishing Mrs. Barkly well and I quickly ducked behind the curtain into Jim's cubicle.

It turned out that Jim had some glass embedded in his arm and was instructed to wear a neck brace for whiplash. He was soon on the mend and I'm glad that his favorite car hadn't been involved. Rather it was a rental car driven by a fellow employee.

A Post Script:

At last I learned: This "NEAT NICK" is more
at home in a bank than in a classroom because
there when you're done, you're done.

Ending tidal wave #1 in Champaign-Urbana-St. Joseph, IL with a paying job proved to be a good way to rest up from all the craziness that proceeded it before being caught up in tidal wave #2 in Clemson, SC.

Chapter 16

ODE TO A SLIPPERY SLUG
1980S

The "Red Baron," our faithful canoe, sat quietly waiting in the woods thirty feet from Turtle Island as we busied ourselves with work on our son-in-law's summer camp in New Hampshire. There was much work to be done as we began to clean up after a hurricane which struck the small island in Lake Wentworth. Cutting up pine trees which lay strewn about was the biggest job, but work was also needed on the buildings.

One day as Bob and Ken cut the trees into logs and split them into fire wood, Peggy and I loaded them into the wheelbarrow and stacked them for later use in the stove and the fireplace. We piled them neatly five feet high and as the pile grew we became exhausted, but we also grew more pleased by how each stack as the logs formed an attractive wall. Two hours later, Ken came to the house for a drink and noticed our effort.

He stopped dead in his tracks and exclaimed, "Oh, No! This won't do! I told you not to stack the logs in a way that would block the view of the lake. I'm sorry, but you have to restack them in another place."

Disappointed and angry with ourselves, we at once started to move the pile to another location. After another two hours, we finally had the logs relocated to a more appropriate place. We were almost sick from exhaustion and after receiving approval from the men, we jumped into the lake to cool off.

At the end of our eight days of vacation and labor, we loaded the canoe on top of the car and took off for our next vacation spot in Acadia National Park in Maine. Suddenly, some weird creature hit the windshield, "kerplunk." I quickly grabbed a pen and paper and was inspired to write the following message:

****

"SLOPPY"

"One warm, sunny, summer day, Sloppy, a slippery slug slipped and slithered slowly, slyly, and subsequently unnoticed into our lives by way of the "Red Baron." As we drove northeastward toward the rocky coast of Maine, Sloppy was suddenly forced to reveal his presence. For hours he had clung precariously inside his hideout, but the continual gale of wind weakened his resistance. No longer able to withstand the force thrust upon him, he lost his grip and catapulted into mid-air and smashed against the van windshield.

Surviving the crash, but slightly smashed, he regained his hold on life as he struggled to also regain his dignity. Slowly he painfully slithered up the windshield against time and tremendous odds trying to inch his way back toward his shelter in the canoe which rode atop the car traveling at fifty miles an hour.

Leaving a trail of entrails behind, he managed to climb eighteen lengths where at last, beaten by overwhelming odds, he thrust his head forward, took one last breath, whispered a final request and relinquished his spirit.

Since we had been unable to assist our stowaway in his struggle to survive, we none the less promised to fulfill his death wish. Sloppy, the slug, expressed great remorse for having abandoned his native New Hampshire lake shore and longed to be buried in the soil from whence he had sprung.

From Acadia National Park a week later, the owners of Turtle Island received the following note and package:

****

"Inside, you will find encased in a plastic coffin, the remains of one repentant, dried out and not so slippery slug named Sloppy. Please bury him in the woods, near the water, across from Turtle Island from whence he had mistakenly departed. May Sloppy, the slippery slug, rest in peace."

Chapter 17

TIDAL WAVE # TWO

Bob's dream came to fruition when he was invited to be Dean of the College of Liberal Arts at Clemson University in Clemson S.C. and, of course, that meant I joined him in the adventure. Finally, we were going to experience hills, mountains, lakes and ocean instead of corn and soy beans fields in flat, land-locked scenery.

The tidal wave of activity began as soon as the moving van was unloaded and everything was put away at our new home at 110 Strode Circle. Since Clemson was so much smaller than Champaign/Urbana, Illinois we immediately felt part of an intimate community of "believers" in Clemson University's mission and the city's future. Everything centered around the University. Due to Bob's leadership position we (along with other new College Deans of Engineering, Nursing, Science and Commerce) were welcomed with open arms and hearts by true Southern hospitality. The residents understood that the changes ahead would affect their lives, but they were excited about the possibilities. Bob and I joined the Clemson administration as a "team" and were caught in the high expectations and the excitement that throbbed around us regarding the changes which lay ahead.

Clemson, SC is a charming college town located in the Piedmont on Lake Hartwell. The winding, hilly, tree-lined streets and a long, but narrow lake, wove through the community and 25 miles beyond. The water was warm and the countless coves encouraged us to swim and boat twelve months of the year. For we two Illini, this was truly a personal delight and a precious treasure.

Our lives immediately became caught up with all aspects and personalities associated with the College of Liberal Arts-professors, staff, students and alumni as well as University administrators across campus. Also, after celebrating our first Mass at St. Andrew's Catholic Church, we acquired many loving friends among the parishioners who soon integrated us into the life of the parish administered by the Paulist Fathers. Throughout the city and within our neighborhood, friendships fell into place as residents drew us into their lives and welcomed us into their homes.

Life in Clemson proved to be a process of becoming part of a very large family which moved together for the benefit of the entire community. Town and gown were as one as we cheered the Clemson football team onto victory in the Fall, followed by other sports teams throughout the year. We also joined the community as residents participated in all the cultural events and educational opportunities sponsored by the University.

Bob's efforts, along with the newly formed Department of the Performing Arts within the College of Liberal Arts and a generous donation from alumnus, Robert Brooks, culminated in building THE BROOKS CENTER, a $12.5 million dollar performing arts complex. The Brooks Center was named after this alumnus. This long sought accomplishment was welcomed by Clemson students, faculty, administration, alumnae, residents and friends from neighboring communities. In addition, due to the efforts of many wise, prudent and hardworking leaders, the University at large grew into an outstanding institution which is now known for its many academic, scholarly, research and athletic pursuits.

Although I was proud to participate along with Bob in these and other ventures at the University, I had other "fish to fry" as I became enmeshed in the spiritual life of St. Andrew's Parish and beyond. What a great group of priests and parishioners!

My involvement included leadership in the Charismatic Prayer group, serving as Lector, Eucharistic Minister at Mass and to the sick, volunteering at Clemson Downs (a local assisted living facility) and the Clemson Little Theater. I received training as a Spiritual Director and formed a group to study the writings of Luisa Piccarreta on Living in the Divine Will. These efforts filled my days along with entertaining University friends, staff and others; enjoying lake activities, traveling with Bob to conferences and meetings around the country and overseas; auditing college classes and completing a correspondence course with The Institute of Children's Literature. That course got my writing career off to a start as I began creating children's stories as I watched boats speed past my study window which overlooked Lake Hartwell. I also enjoyed auditing a variety of classes at the University. What a stimulating place in which to live and work!

Life in Clemson developed into a non-stop existence of cultural, educational, spiritual, creative and physical activities along with a very full social calendar as we luxuriated in temperate weather conditions. I felt thrilled when an occasional snowfall came our way and I breathed a sigh of both sorrow and joy as the snow paused only a few days to add excitement, charm and challenge to our lives. Life in Clemson was incredible. We stayed there to work and to play until 2000 when we retired to Florida.

Chapter 18

ALONE IN ROME AND PARIS
1983 CLEMSON, SC

It was on a whim that I found myself on a flight to France and Italy. I couldn't miss the opportunity to visit Peggy who was doing research in Paris, her beloved city. It was 1983 and I had never traveled to Europe, but it wouldn't be a problem. After all, Peggy had traveled alone all over Europe on a Eurail Pass in 1975 when she was twenty-one. If she could do that then, I, now a mother of three-grown children, could certainly do the same at fifty-three.

I flew from Atlanta, GA into Brussels, Belgium, made a tricky transfer from the airport to the railroad station and caught a train to Paris where Peggy met me at the Garde de Nord Station. We took off immediately for a walking tour through the city. It was wonderful to have my own loving daughter as my guide, especially since she spoke fluent French and was free that day. We ended our tour by going to Peggy's dormitory after dinner so I could meet her friends. After our short visit, she put me on a city bus and sent me back to my hotel across town. I returned safely and fell asleep exhausted.

The next day I investigated the neighborhood shops and churches, grabbed a snack from a delicatessen to eat in my room and crawled into bed early because the following day it was off on the train to Liseiux, France to visit the home of St. Therese, her shrine and her convent. Her incorruptible body encased in glass was beautiful and to be where she had lived was inspirational. I stopped in the Convent chapel once again before I returned to the train station. This time I heard heavenly singing which filled the space. It turned out to be the Sisters practicing Gregorian chant hidden behind an ornate grill and not a choir of angels. When I reported my safe return to Paris, Peggy was elated.

The next day I once again walked the city streets in search of sights which interested me. At 4:00 I arrived at Notre Dame Cathedral and settled down for prayer in this famous and inspiring church, but was surprised to find the church almost empty, -a perfect time and place to sit by myself to pray and to study the interior. I jumped when I felt someone touch my shoulder and whisper in my ear, "I'm sorry, Madame, but you will have to leave. We are closing the church doors, but you may return at 6:00 p.m."

For the next two hours I wandered around the neighborhood and visited many places of interest and joined in prayer with different groups of people. At 6:00 I returned to Notre Dame only to find the place packed with hundreds of tourists and religious. In the center aisle, from the altar to the back row of pews, stood tables end to end with chairs on one side. "What in heaven's name is going on here?" I asked an English speaking native after I had inched myself through the crowd up to the altar area on the far left of the Sanctuary.

"This is the Diocese of Paris' Holy Year Celebration. The Archbishop with all the Diocesan clergy will celebrate the Eucharist together. I'm delighted that you are here to share in this holy event," she said and gave me a hug. The Mass was offered with great pomp and circumstance. When it finally ended almost two hours later, I returned to my hotel floating on cloud nine which kept me from feeling my very sore feet and tired body. In fact, I don't even remember how I found my way back to the hotel room.

The following morning Peggy accompanied me to the train station to catch the train for an overnight trip to Rome. I could see her peering in the train window as we waved goodbye to one another with tears in our eyes. Unfortunately, I had taken a seat in a smoke filled car. I soon escaped and huddled in the passageway until I met a friendly lady who joined me in locating a non-smoking car. We became instant friends. She was a citizen of Rome and spoke fluent English. When we reached the city, she offered to share her cab, but I declined saying, "I don't want you to go out of your way. I'm OK. I'll just grab another cab. Thanks! I've enjoyed our sharing. I hope we will meet again."

The cab driver was very friendly which was fine until he said he would carry my suitcase into the hotel and see that my reservation had been made to my satisfaction. That was very kind, but I made sure that he didn't catch my name or my room number. The room they assigned me was located on an inner court so when the boisterous noise and horn honking began outside that evening, I couldn't see what was happening. The commotion went on for hours. In desperation I called the desk to find out when it would stop.

"I'm so sorry Madame, but Rome has just won the international soccer tournament and this celebration will last until early morning. Perhaps, you may want to enjoy a bottle of wine and try to ignore the ruckus."

I did as he suggested and I was also resigned to ignore the shouting and the clanging of dishes in the hotel kitchen which reached me through my courtyard window. When I awoke early the next morning, I was relieved to find that the revelers had exhausted themselves and gone home leaving a monster of a mess in their wake.

Today at last, it was time for me to see St. Peter's and all its intrigue and treasures. Like most travelers, I was overwhelmed by its vast and beautiful interior! Fortunately, since I was alone I could just sit quietly or wander as I pleased looking at and listening to the sights and sounds that surrounded me. When I took the elevator to the gift shop on the roof, I discovered that if I climbed 325 steps to the Dome I would reach a spot on the rim of the Dome where I could see Rome and all the buildings and grounds of Vatican City. What an incredible sight! The climb had been exhausting, but the descent seemed more precarious as I carefully placed my feet on each step. The steps seemed especially narrow as they wound down to the flat roof below. I clenched the railing tightly for fear of falling forward or tripping on the stair's edge. The height was also dizzying. When I reached the roof, exhausted in body and on shaky knees, I took a deep breath and breathed a sigh of relief. This was an adventure I had not expected. The gift shop proved to be a world full of captivating items, but with limited cash and my inability to carry many objects, I chose well and wisely.

That night I treated myself to dinner on the roof of a nearby hotel which overlooked St. Peter's Square. A wedding celebration gave the dinner hour a festive atmosphere as I struggled to decide what to eat. I finally gave up studying the menu and ordered my dinner by pointing to the food on the table closest to me. The waiter was kind, but impatient as I'm sure he knew my tip for his service would likely be inadequate. As I slowly consumed that delicious dinner, I nourished every sight and sound of Rome at night, - it was truly a day and a night to remember.

As I left the hotel the next morning, the clerk called me aside and asked, "Mrs. Waller, what time are you planning check out of your room?"

Shocked, I said, "Oh, I'm not leaving until tomorrow."

"Madame, I'm sorry, but your room reservation ends at 11:00 am today."

"But what am I to do. I have a ticket for the Papal Audience today and my train doesn't leave until tomorrow night."

"Well," he said, "Pack your bags and bring everything down to me. I will put them in a locked storage room. Meanwhile, I will find you a room nearby for tonight."

Trusting, I followed his instructions, left my possessions, including the items I had purchased in the gift shop and enjoyed the Papal Audience for the next few hours while trying to ignore my predicament. The Papal audience was awesome!

Returning to my hotel the desk clerk said, "I have made you a reservation for tonight at a hotel just around the corner."

"Thank you very much. I'm sorry I was mistaken about the length of my stay at your fine hotel and had to trouble you," I said as I gathered up my things and departed.

Well, it turned out to be a very long way to the corner and walking proved a bit precarious as I dodged Fiats parked on the sidewalks, pedestrians hurrying from one place to another, cars speeding along with horns blaring and people shouting to each other. At last I arrived at the appointed hotel and explained my problem to the desk clerk with great assurance as he checked his big register.

"I'm sorry, Madame, but I don't see a reservation for you and we have no room available for tonight. If you would like, we could hold your things for you in a locked storage room while you check for a room at another hotel nearby."

Downcast, I did as the man suggested and proceeded to search for a room without any luck. Someone suggested that I take a bus to the train station and change tomorrow's ticket for that night. The bus ride was nerve wracking as the driver constantly leaned out the bus window and shouted obscenities at the traffic and the pedestrians. When I finally reached the train station I tried hard to explain my problem to the reservations clerk in English, but he ignored me and then waved me away.

Now I was really scared. I grabbed a bus back to the hotel where I had left my bags. In tears I explained to the man that I was unable to find a room and the effort to change my ticket was to no avail.

He consulted his reservation book again and consulted with his manager. When he returned smiling, my heart jumped for joy as he explained that I could book an unused storage room which had a bed. I was both surprised and relieved to find it to be a very large empty room overlooking a busy street, - a room with a view at last. The next day, I remembered that the Paulist Fathers served a parish near the train station, so I hauled my possessions onto a bus headed to Santa Suzanna Catholic Church. The priests gladly offered to park my belongings while I spent the day investigating the area nearby. After dinner, relieved and elated, I recovered my baggage and hurried to catch the train for an overnight ride back to Paris and to Peggy. This time I made sure that I found a seat in a non-smoking car. The ride proved uneventful and Peggy waved enthusiastically when she saw me emerge from the train safe and sound.

We shared lunch and she laughed as I related my adventures. She took me to where my train for Brussels would depart, but left me there to fend for myself as she hurried off to keep an appointment with her editor. Since I was now a "seasoned" traveler, I was anxious to travel unescorted on the train to Brussels so I could relax and reflect. However, but fortunately, it turned out that a French College Student joined me in my compartment. He spoke English and we chatted happily. When an announcement came across the speaker several hours later, he packed up his things and put on his coat as he said, "I thought you were going to Brussels."

"Oh, I am," I replied sitting there complacently.

"Well, then you had better hurry and get ready to change cars. This car is returning to Paris. Your car to Brussels is three cars ahead. Hurry! I'll help you catch it before it pulls out."

With that he grabbed my suitcase and we raced down the tracks. When we reached the proper car he tossed my bag onto the train and boosted me up the steps as the train began inching forward. I waved joyfully as the kind student disappeared into the distance. Thank you, God. You knew better what I needed than I did. Wouldn't Peggy have been surprised if I inadvertently returned to Paris and ended up on her dormitory doorstep.

At dinner in the hotel a "nice" man asked me if he could join me. This frightened me, so I declined his invitation, gobbled up my food, hurried to my room and bolted the door. The next morning I hurried out of the hotel hoping to miss seeing that gentleman again. I boarded my flight to the United States. Hours later I arrived safely in Atlanta, GA and ran into the waiting arms of my relieved and loving husband.

Bob and I prayed a prayer of thanksgiving for my safe return and Peggy could concentrate once again on her research. I'll never ever forget that adventure, - and I did it myself!

Chapter 19

"OUT ON A LIMB"
1984 CLEMSON, SC

Living in upstate South Carolina afforded us several choices of lakes to explore. Of them all, Lake Jocasee proved the most intriguing. It was located the farthest from Clemson, high up in the Piedmont with isolated access. The morning was cool and a bit overcast as we arrived in the vicinity of the lake and searched for the access point which friends had described. It took a bit of searching, but we finally discovered the boat ramp and launched "The Red Baron."

The wake of our canoe caused the only movement in the water as it glided silently across the quiet lake. Nary a breeze nor a human soul could be felt or seen. We paddled for twenty minutes not even whispering a word. The silence and seclusion seemed almost mystical: what peace, what beauty, what serenity!

Unaware of a sound far off in the distance, we were startled when suddenly two fighter jets dove out of the clouds above us, sped past and shot back into the overcast sky and disappeared, never to be seen again. It took us a few minutes to compose ourselves before we proceeded deeper into the lake. *

Again silence enveloped us. Far ahead we spotted a boat sitting at anchor, but no one appeared to be anywhere in sight. When we reached the abandoned craft, we thought at first that the occupants were scuba diving, but there was no evidence to be found which suggested that possibility. Bewildered, we paddled away as we said a prayer that the owners were alive and well.

After paddling another quarter hour we heard the sound of rushing water and realized the spillway was ahead. Going near or even close to the edge could spell disaster as "The Red Baron" could be sucked in by the swift current and tossed onto the spillway and the rock laden stream below. Luckily, we acted in time and soon found ourselves paddling toward a beach.

As we approached land, we heard women and children laughing, playing and swimming off the beach with no men in sight, no boat and no cars. How did they get there? Then, we made the connection between the abandoned boat, the women and the children. We surmised that there must have been a second boat which had gone for help in regard to the abandoned boat. Relieved that perhaps we had solved that mystery and to have survived our adventures, we waved to them and headed back to locate the access ramp once again.

We never ventured to Lake Jocassee again. Instead, we were content to canoe in the less challenging Lake Keowee where we took our chances with all the skiddos racing about and the quieter Lake Hartwell right in our own back yard.

*Subsequently, we ascertained the pilots in the jets were practicing a bombing run on the dam.

Chapter 20

RETREATS SOMETIMES LEAD TO MORE THAN HOLINESS

1983 THE HOUSE AT 145 FOLGER STREET, CLEMSON, SC observed the following:

One day a large moving van backed into my driveway. Strong men LOADED the van with furniture, a few appliances, tons of clothes and hundreds of boxes. When the van drove away I felt naked. No pictures hung on my walls. No curtains graced my windows. No children ran up and down my stairs. Now, only silence wrapped its arms around me like the cobwebs which clung to my siding. I'd been abandoned.

The next day, I noticed a large FOR SALE sign in my yard.

After that, I wasn't lonely anymore because day after day for a few months I listened to everyone insult me. Women complained about my kitchen. Men complained about my basement and garage. Children complained about my staircases and loose banisters. Though everyone loved my lake view and location, nobody liked my condition. Little by little the number of house buyers dwindled to a dribble. Then, for almost two years, no one came. There was just that dirty FOR SALE sign out in front. I sat empty, cold, lonely and miserable.

OCTOBER 1985—A RETREAT AT
ST. ANDREWS CLEMSON, SC

The Fall day proved to be perfect and the retreat inspiring, but God had something much bigger on His mind that day than my growing in sanctity. In fact, the day was so perfect that at break-time I strolled through the wooded neighborhood passed lovely homes and down winding streets. My first right turn led me to a dead end where I suddenly found myself face to face with a lake and a forlorn looking house that cried out for help. A faded FOR SALE sign stood among the high grass and weeds on this most choice piece of land at 145 Folger Street.

Its windows and screens, gutters and downspouts, siding and roofing, lawns and landscaping and much more needed not only love, but some major hours of labor and cold, hard cash. With my heart filled with desire and creative ideas, not with "holy thoughts," I tried hard to concentrate on the retreat subject. Instead, I watched the clock anxiously waiting to call the realtor with a million questions concerning the object of my desire.

For years, I had dreamed of living on a lake, in the woods on a hill. It's no wonder that this house grabbed my imagination. Besides, 145 Folger Street was located near the Catholic Church, campus town and Clemson University, -including the Tiger football stadium. If we added a dock, we would be able to hear bands playing and the fans cheering the Tigers on to victory as the sounds echoed off Lake Hartwell. We would also be able to watch the boats cruise by our house on the way to the football games and, if we bought a boat, we could join them.

The next morning, when the realtor unlocked the door to my dream house, I knew this was to be our house. "I love it!" I exclaimed as we toured the interior.

"What?" she said looking at me as if I had "lost my mind."

"You love this house? Do you realize it has been on the market for two years. The Dean of Architecture bought it when it first went on sale, but almost immediately he decided to resell." Even if she lost the sale, she was determined to help me come to my senses. After all, she was a friend.

That evening, as the sun set over the lake, Bob came with me to take a look.

SURPRISED! THE HOUSE HEARD THE MAN SAY TO THE REALTOR:

"My wife is right. This sad, wonderful house is just what we've dreamed of owning. THIS IS THE PERFECT HOUSE FOR US and we'll have it beautiful again in no time."

We signed on the dotted line and began packing boxes in preparation for our move during the Christmas holidays. This very untidy house required hours of cleaning before we could move in and settle down. For three weeks, from early morning until dark during the 1985 Christmas Holidays we swept, scrubbed, vacuumed, washed windows/blinds and discarded all sorts of trash. When we were exhausted from that work, we returned to our Strode Circle house and packed boxes until midnight, then dropped into bed and fell fast asleep.

JANUARY 1986 THE HOUSE SHARES ITS JOYFUL MEMORIES

On January 3rd, a moving van backed into my driveway. Strong men UNLOADED furniture, appliances and myriads of boxes. At last I smiled with joy and excitement. Someone loved me in spite of my broken plaster, rusted sinks, damaged walls, filthy woodwork, my defaced fireplace and smelly, stained carpeting.

During the following nine months serious work began to change me. When they scrubbed and painted my walls, I squirmed and giggled.

When by hand they scrapped, picked, sanded and buffed the years of old paint drips and smudges off my hardwood floors, I winced, cringed, and then smiled.

When they hung some wallpaper, added curtains and blinds to my windows, and replaced the screens, I felt cozy and private.

When they hammered a new roof over me, I got a headache.

When they swept my chimney, I sneezed.

When they capped my chimney, I gave a sigh of relief.

When they scrubbed and stained my deck, I felt cleaner.

When they dressed me in white vinyl with blue shutters and added new gutters and downspouts, I felt eloquent.

When, after months of blood, sweat and tears had been spent on my interior, the time came to replace my ugly grass with sod, to landscape my yard, to tear the grapevines off the oak trees and dogwoods in my woods and to plant azaleas and flowers in my gardens.

Then, I proudly watched as friends and strangers stopped to admire the "new me" both inside and out.

NOW THE MAN AND HIS WIFE CAN ENJOY

A flaming western sky at sunset and diamond-like sparkles of sunlight dancing on the water;

Boats and water skiers speeding by and fishermen trolling along the shore;

A swim after a hot summer day or a ride on the lake with family or friends; or candidates for college positions.

A refreshing breeze blowing across the porch and the deck;

Squirrels frolicking about the woods;

Picturesque views from every vantage point;

Wonderful neighbors and a stable, quiet neighborhood;

Cozy spaces for intimate conversations and a good traffic flow for large crowds;

Hardwood floors, real plaster walls; a house with style, grace and charm;

Towering hardwoods, flowering dogwoods and flaming azaleas;

Short walks to town, to churches and to campus passing by beautiful homes with countless azalea beds

A mountain in view during fall, winter and early spring;

A house filled with warm sunlight during the winter, yet a house shaded and cool in the summer;

Guests sharing fun, food and conversation and family visiting from afar;

And always serenity, beauty, and comfort inside and outside.

I TRULY AM THE HOUSE OF THEIR DREAMS."

Chapter 21

TRANSFORMING OUR DREAM HOUSE
1985 DECEMBER

Here is what it took!

Before the final purchase contract was signed, we spent over 300 hours of morning to night labor during the two-week Christmas holiday break just to make our dream house tolerably livable.

We were faced with broken plaster; filthy carpeting; dirty walls and woodwork; tarnished door knobs; a soap-caked tub, shower stall and sinks; broken toilets; crude, ugly basement stairs that led to a smelly, filthy, unkempt basement; a rusted-out kitchen sink cabinet; and mildew stained interior and exterior walls. These were only some the items which stared back at us.

We slowly started to move small items into our dream house on Christmas Day 1985 with no help from family, friends, colleagues or neighbors, many of whom were busy traveling or celebrating the Christmas break with family or friends. In fact, no one even knew we were planning to move anywhere.

In January 1986, the final papers were signed and the house was ours. Now the real work could begin. Each morning, I dressed in my grey T shirt and grey sweat pant, which would continue to be my uniform each day. I tackled the smaller renovations as Bob tackled a new load of responsibilities at Clemson University under the recently selected president. He joined me after school each day and on the weekends when we worked from breakfast to bedtime. Twelve months later we had completed the following projects ourselves:

While Bob worked at the University, I painted all the walls and woodwork. After dinner and on weekends together, we wallpapered the kitchen and bathrooms; repaired and tiled the kitchen and bathroom floors. We installed chair rails throughout the house; cleaned years of crud from bathtub and shower stall; replaced toilets and sinks; re-screened the porch; cleaned and re-stained the wood deck; built a new basement staircase with the help of Tom and the grandchildren who acted as "board sitters." We removed crayon marks from the recreation room brick fireplace; scoured and painted the basement walls and floors, carpeted these floors and later carpeted the dock. A ramp was also built to anchor the dock to the shore. In the midst of all this activity Bob and I battled the underbrush in the woods and ripped grape vines from the trees in the overgrown quarter acre of woods beside the house and between the house and the lake. All this work was done working up hill.

Then, when all the work in the house was completed, we ripped up the filthy carpeting, including all the carpet strips, tacks and staples, only to discover that the previous owners had carpeted over a whole houseful of paint splatters and paint splotches which by now had been ground into the hardwood floors. Since we couldn't call in a professional sander because of the dust sanding would cause, the only solution to the problem was to pick, scrape, sand and rub the drops and smudges of paint out of existence. On our hands and knees, hour after hour, for weeks we worked until our mission was accomplished.

Together, the large living/dining room alone took eighty hours to restore. It took many more hours to match some replacement floor boards near the fireplace to the 40-year old flooring. Work on the hardwood floors turned out to be more exhausting than any one of our other major projects. But, we did it!

With the inside finally under control other major eye sores cried out for attention.

We constructed shelves for storage and set up a decent workroom in the basement; painted all exterior doors and windows and replaced the screens; hung blinds and curtains on twenty eight windows; and refinished furniture. Bob installed steps behind the house to make it easier to climb the hill to and from the lake. With help from son, Tom and the grandchildren, who again acted as "board sitters," a ramp to extend the dock further out into the lake was constructed.

Professionals designed and implemented landscape changes in the front yard; installed a sprinkler system; placed new black shingles on the roof; covered the pea green asbestos siding with white vinyl siding and blue/gray shutters; replaced the aluminum sliding door to the deck with a wooden one; delivered all new kitchen appliances; refinished the bathtub; reupholstered several chairs and couches; sealed the long, wide driveway; cleaned and removed moss from the brick walkway and steps; dug up the 40-year old oil tank from the side yard; and hung new gutters and downspouts. A carpenter changed cabinet doors and counter tops in the kitchen and bathrooms and he also added a new cabinet. New pieces of furniture, white wool area rugs, pictures and other accessories were purchased. The entire project took us one full year to complete. We lived with and entertained in the house in spite of the work in progress and the mess it created. Everyone thoroughly enjoyed the cozy and attractive "new" home as much as we did. Many remarked, "Let us know before you put this house on the market because we'd sure love to buy it."

With the work's completion, the house stood clean and sparkling amid the very tall oak and hickory trees, flowering dogwoods and soft pines. A carpet of new green grass in the front of the house welcomed visitors. A pristine forest and the lake on the back side of the house charmed them as they viewed it from the deck or descended through the woods to the boat and carpeted dock on Lake Hartwell. The sunsets on the lake each evening were delightful as was boating and swimming off the dock and the boat. This made all the work worthwhile.

However, on our return from a trip to California we were shocked to find that the woods looked bare and boring. "What is wrong? What has happened to our beautiful woods?" As we walked down to the dock we began to see the problem. It seems that while we were away, beavers had descended on our property and had stolen thirteen of our wild flowering dogwoods with which to build themselves a dam somewhere. The pointed trunks of missing trees were a dead giveaway. They'd gnawed down and hauled them away without anyone being the wiser. Oh, well. Dams are as important to beavers as beautiful woods are to humans.

When the house went up for sale seven years later, it was sold even before it was on the market. This truly was a labor of love which paid off in countless joys and pleasures.

Chapter 22

REMEMBERING SISTER DORIS
1987-1993 CLEMSON, SC

For six years, we shared our three-story home on the lake with a most incredible woman named Doris. When Sr. Doris was hired at our parish as the Director of Religious Education (DRE), we invited her to share our home. The recreation room on ground level provided her with a living room/bedroom, a wood burning fireplace and privacy. Doris, an avid swimmer, had just spent a number of years ministering in Alaska. So, a room which faced the lake and was a short walk out the door and down the hill to the dock, proved ideal. Having to share a bath and the kitchen on the first floor was no problem for this enthusiastic "young 55-year old" Dominican Sister.

Doris was hired as the DRE, but soon was up to her neck in a wealth of projects and activities which cried out for attention. The first project involved getting a group of women to clean and organize every drawer, cabinet, closet and room in the chapel, the church and the social hall. At first the parish priests panicked as we went merrily on our way pursuing our projects, fearing that all their favorite and much needed treasures would go missing. Soon they realized that we had not discarded any important paper or item, but had only destroyed all the clutter which had hidden them. Peace and tranquility soon returned.

For years no one person with authority had been in charge of the buildings. Each parishioner or staff member had simply done their "thing" as they saw fit until most everything, including the kitchen, had become a mare's nest. With Doris we finally had someone with the authority, the energy, the "know how" and the leadership skill to tackle the mess and to solve the problem. Our efforts were welcomed by both the staff and the parishioners and Sister Doris gained a well-deserved, positive reputation.

Sister was a talented and most energetic laborer for the Lord. Filled daily with constant prayer and study, there wasn't anything she couldn't or wouldn't do to get a job done. For the Liturgy, she played and sang with the guitar and helped the young people get involved. She even performed liturgical dance on occasion. Her Religious Education volunteers gained wisdom and knowledge from a director who knew Church theology as well as the teaching skills they needed to pass the Catholic Faith onto to their students.

And on top of all that Sr. Doris played, laughed, and constantly taught everyone she met. She is a born teacher and an inspiration. From 6:00 am to Midnight she labored and played. When not officially engaged in work for the parish, the parishioners, the college students and others, one could find her climbing mountains, cross country skiing, swimming, running, dancing and singing. We enjoyed her spontaneous lunches at our home while counseling, feeding and entertaining students who enjoyed her company or with groups about to embark on some adventure. Living in South Carolina with Lake Hartwell and Clemson University at her fingertips, there was no time for boredom.

The best part of having Doris live with us was the fact that we were brought alive daily as she shared her life and thoughts with us at dinner; in the evening as we ate popcorn and enjoyed a glass of wine; as we watched her come and go with the Parish youth and grownups who shared her activities; as well as the many times we swam off the dock and boated around the lake together.

At home we learned to live as doors slammed as Doris hurried from one place or one activity to another and to hear Sister talking to us before she even came into view. She loved to discuss and argue about almost anything "in the news." Her mind was a beehive of thoughts, opinions and experiences which she shared with us. Even the challenging statements and subjects she introduced into our conversations sometimes ended in heated debates which helped us to grow. We managed to tolerate her arriving home just after we had finished a back-breaking project and asking why we were perspiring so much. You see, Doris never perspired. And last, but not least, we were aghast as we watched her consume jalapeno peppers and pepper juice in and on everything she ate. It seems that while ministering in New Mexico she became addicted to HOT food. To her, food without jalapeno peppers or their juice tasted boring.

We loved her presence in our lives, all her fun-loving ways, her kindnesses and generosity toward everyone. I personally appreciated the time she spent editing my latest essay or story and how she supported my writing endeavors. Over those six years we were stretched, entertained, informed, matured and maybe, grew in virtue through this experience of sharing our home and our "fortune" with Sister Doris, who remains our best friend even many years later.

Chapter 23

BEAUTY OR BEAST?
1988 JANUARY CLEMSON, SC

South Carolina is not a state that worries too much about blizzards. However, one night the weather report was full of dire warnings of a severe storm which was expected to bring a combination of sleet, wind, and serious snow to the Upstate. We were warned to take precautions. So, when I fell asleep that night my mind was preoccupied with the question: "Will it or won't it?"

THEN MORNING ARRIVED AND THE
FOLLOWING MEDITATION WAS BORN:

I awoke from a deep and dreamful sleep, warm and secure. All was quiet and dim—no sun, no voices, no sounds outside or in.

Then, I remembered the question on everyone's mind the night before. Would the blizzard come or would it be delayed? Perhaps, it wouldn't come at all. There was no way to know except to crack the blinds and peek outside.

There lay the earth blanketed in white: all its imperfections covered and miraculously transformed—the magic, the mystery of a virgin snowfall with its power to grip the human soul and spirit, power to bring loved ones and strangers together or to separate them for a time or forever.

My mind was torn with indecision—to remain safe inside or to reach out to the challenge of winter. My emotions fluctuated between joy and fear, between wonder and anxiety.

I felt joyful at the thought of being home alone, nestled by the warm fireplace with time to be creative or unproductive; fear for those caught unaware and anxious for those who must risk their lives to rescue them; wonderment at the beauty which our heavenly Father had wrapped around us: His all-embracing love; His tenderness; His grace gently falling upon his creation blanketing our mistakes and our transgressions. "Though your sins be like scarlet, they may become white as snow," He promised (Isaiah 1:18).

I feared for those trapped, lost or alone; for those without heat, without food, or without anyone to care; for those too old, too sick or too young; for those caught in this tragic beauty of life because they cared enough to risk all as they reached out to others less fortunate.

I rejoiced with students whose classes were canceled and for those healthy and energetic enough to play in the magic which had fallen; -building snowmen, forts and castles; making snow angels; hiking, skiing, and frolicking freely; neighbors meeting as they shoveled snow, retrieved automobiles, and shared the excitement and the tragedies of the moment.

Snowfall is a time for poets and authors to compose, for artists and photographers to capture, for lovers to embrace. It's a time for fireplaces, popcorn, and cocoa; for stories, laughter and memories; for skis, sleds and toboggans. It's a time for good deeds, new friendships, and trust. It's a time of stress and relaxation, elation and depression, repentance and forgiveness, challenge and creativity. It's a time for wonder.

What other touch of the Creator's hand brings with it such a blend of blessing and tragedy? What other time of year so confuses our emotions, stimulates our inner being, and interrupts our plans, reminding us of our lack of control.

Oh Lord, how we need this mystery, this challenge, this delight. Without it we tend to forget You and Your purpose in creating us—to give You honor, praise and worship. With snow, You remind us of Your awesome goodness and power and You call us to recognize our dependence on You and our interdependence on one another, friend and stranger.

Perhaps, Snow is both Beauty and Beast.

Chapter 24

TO WALK WHERE PAUL WALKED
JULY 1990 CLEMSON ALUMNI CRUISE

AN INVITATION:

To climb the Areopagus where St. Paul delivered this address: "Men of Athens, I note that in every respect you are scrupulously religious. As I walked around looking at your shrines, I even discovered an altar inscribed 'To a God Unknown.' Now what you are thus worshipping in ignorance I intend to make [Him] known to you...."

To experience the ancient ruins of Ephesus where Paul upset the Silversmith's trade selling silver statues of the goddess Diana because so many Ephesians had turned away from Diana and had embraced Jesus because of Paul's preaching.

To pass by Corinth where St. Paul taught for a year and a half after the Lord encouraged him in a vision saying: "Do not be afraid. Go on speaking and do not be silenced for I am with you...."

****

"How would you like to take a cruise to Greece, Turkey, Russia and Italy?" Bob telephoned to ask me while I was visiting my parents in Florida

"Don't be silly, we can't afford such an extraordinary vacation?" I replied impatiently.

"Don't worry. The trip won't cost us anything. The Clemson University Alumni Association has invited us to serve as host couple for a twelve-day cruise on the Golden Odyssey, a Costa Cruise Liner. I will be required to present lectures about how the United States was involved with the places we will visit and you can do that dramatic reading you like so well about St. Paul in Ephesus."

"So what do you think about that for a surprise?"

"Incredible, fantastic, let's do it!" I shouted, and so we did.

THE TRIP:

Early on July 18, 1990 we flew to Atlanta, GA to catch our flight to Frankfort, Germany and then on to Athens, Greece. Unfortunately a severe thunderstorm delayed our departure. Frank and Hilda, our charming 85-year old, experienced, cane carrying travel companions joined us for the three-hour wait until our flight resumed. However, when we arrived at the Frankfort airport our plane to Athens had already departed, so they booked us on a flight to Munich, Germany where we were delayed again for quite some time. Finally, over six hours behind schedule we reached Athens. Naturally, our luggage was nowhere to be found. The baggage handler suggested we take a cab to the other Athens airport, but to no avail. It was near midnight July 19th when we boarded the "Golden Odyssey." We expected "someone" to be glad we'd finally arrived, but no one seemed to have even missed us and the members of our group had long been asleep.

When we inquired about the room assignments for Bob's lectures and my presentation, which we presumed had been made, it turned out that, instead of a private room, we were to use the main theatre. All the passengers would be invited to attend. It turned out that a considerable number of the 450 passengers would choose to join our thirty Alumni. Bob presented the man on duty with the Clemson University flag which was to be flown over the cruise ship as we entered the Black Sea. It was after 1:00 am before our business was concluded and we proceeded to locate our stateroom by ourselves.

A blast of freezing air greeted us as the door of our stateroom opened. The thermostat was stuck at 60 and a radio blared in the adjoining stateroom. Without luggage, exhausted and disappointed, we crawled fully clothed into our separate beds wearing the same clothes we'd worn since we left Clemson, SC.

Although the beginning of our maiden voyage may have been comical and challenging, the remaining days proved exciting and orderly as we shared fun-filled days and nights with our Clemson Alumni friends.

A full day of sightseeing preceded our midnight departure from Athens as our ship sailed north through the Aegean Sea, the Dardanelles and the Sea of Marmara. After we sailed pass Istanbul, Turkey and entered the Black Sea, which is true to its name, the captain hoisted our Clemson flag as all the passengers cheered. Later the ship docked at Yalta and later Odessa, Russia.

For Bob, a 20th Century American Historian, Yalta, Russia on the Black Sea was the highlight of the trip. It was thrilling for him as he stood in the conference room where the course of Western Civilization had taken a dramatic turn during World War II. It was especially significant since the year following our trip the Berlin Wall had crumbled. Once again the course of history turned another corner.

After Yalta, we stopped in Odessa, Russia for a brief tour and an extravagant banquet of Russian food. We prayed that the Costa Cruise Line had contributed to the cost of this incredible lunch because we were embarrassed at how little most of us ate. The city was obviously still suffering from a serious depression judging from the sad disrepair of the city's buildings and the lack of merchandise in the store windows, including the food shops.

The "Golden Odyssey" returned to Istanbul where we stopped for the day before sailing along the coast of Asia to Kusadasi/Ephesus, Turkey. While on board ship and before we reached Ephesus, I presented my dramatic reading about that Biblically famous place. The reading concerned St. Paul and the Silversmiths and it also covered the circumstances of this once ancient city at the time Paul taught there. When we arrived at the amphitheater where Paul had spoken, the passengers could now more readily identify with St. Paul's experience and appreciate what the once vibrant city had been like.

For me, a lover of Catholic Church History, Ephesus, Turkey stands out as the highlight of the trip. Here for two years, St. Paul preached and worked as a tent/sail maker. Ephesus, one of the most outstanding ports of its time, now lays abandoned, but not forgotten. The history and the treasures of this once ancient city of 250,000 inhabitants has been laid bare through the painstaking work of archaeologists. Paul's presence in Ephesus is dramatically recorded in Acts 19:1-20:2.

Ephesus is also the place where the Blessed Virgin Mary and St. John had lived. Mary's house, the tomb of St. John and the remains of churches built in their memory stand there today, but our tour did not include going there. It was in Ephesus and on the Greek Island of Patmos that John wrote his Gospel and Revelations. The Ecumenical Council of 421 was held in the Church of the Virgin Mary at Ephesus where the Virgin was officially proclaimed the Mother of God because her Son, Jesus, is Divine.

From Ephesus we stopped briefly at the beautiful Greek Island of Mykonos. Then, sailing passed Athens, the ship entered the narrow Corinth Canal for a three -hour illuminated, midnight passage. In the morning we sailed up the southwest coast of Greece and stopped briefly at the charming Island of Corfu.

Although our cruise ship passed close to the country of Albania in the Bay of Kotor, the Communist controlled government would not allow our foreign ship to dock at its port. Our next port was Dubrovnik, Yugoslavia where we climbed its famous city wall, but since I was frightened by the height of the wall, we never walked the entire distance around the city. A decision I regret.

Our twelve-day adventure climaxed with sightseeing in Venice, Italy. We however, missed both the sightseeing and the gondola-serenade through Venice's charming canals for which tourists spend a fortune. Instead, we spent all our time in Venice exploring the backstreets and alleyways as we searched for an Italian marine flag which we promised to buy for our boat-loving friends back in Clemson. Since our deck boat, named "Eutrapelia" flew a Greek marine flag, Gene & Carolyn insisted they needed an Italian marine flag to fly on their Bayliner runabout. Although the flag search was unsuccessful, we probably saw more of the real Venice than most tourists and the memory of our search is one of the trip's highlights. We brought home a most interesting framed painting on wood which we found hidden in an art gallery on one of the back streets.

The morning we returned to Columbia, SC, Bob checked the phone book for a flag store for one last try. To reach the only flag store in the city required us to walk four miles round trip, down the highway, in ninety degree heat. We bought the last Italian marine flag the proprietor had in stock. Though our friends were delighted that we found the flag, they were also disappointed when they learned that the flag didn't hail from Venice, but from our home state of SC. Nevertheless, it makes a good story and a wonderful memory.

Our cherished memories and our gratitude to the Clemson Alumni Association for the gift of this incredible cruise will remain with us forever.

Chapter 25

A TIDAL WAVE # THREE
2000 THE VILLAGES, FL PART ONE

In 2000, we began the new millenium century by moving to The Villages, Florida and chose a house located on the 8th fairway of the Tierra del Sol golf course in the Village of Palo Alto. We were never sorry about choosing this home even though it was purchased virtually sight unseen. We anticipated retiring to a leisurely life, or so we thought, but soon another tidal wave struck and we were off and running again.

Golf lessons and golfing brought us into the swing of things since it's hard to live in a golf cart community and not play golf virtually for free. Ballroom dance instructions and dances set us moving rhythmically. Clubs are a big part of getting acquainted so we joined the following: Illinois, Chicago, Palo Alto, Italian-American, Irish-American, German-American and dance clubs. We learned to play countless card games and returned at last to playing bridge.

I became involved in the St. Timothy Parish and served as Lector and Eucharistic Minister at Mass, took Communion to the sick and became a leader of the Charismatic Prayer Group. Together we worked on the "Coffee And" Sunday morning social committee. Once again I formed a Divine Will Study group and then a second group to discuss Catholic Christian Spirituality and Scripture.

Bob's attention was drawn to the newly formed Villages College for Life Long Learning where he offered classes in American Political History eight to ten weeks a year with all the necessary preparation that such a commitment required. He relaxed daily by working on his fast growing stamp collection.

When an organ store opened next to the grocery and offered instructions, I bought a used organ and took lessons. Experts say playing the organ is a wonderful way for older folks to keep up their spirits and to train their minds. This became my favorite form of recreation until we moved again.

SLOWING DOWN OR BEING PRODUCTIVE?
2009 THE VILLAGES, FL PART TWO

In 2009, we sold our home on the golf course and bought a two-bedroom condo at FREEDOM POINTE, an Independent Living Facility high rise condominium in The Villages, which provides continuing care. That move eliminated all the yard work and home owner chores. Here, we finally found time to relax and be productive.

The move caused a problem with my organ, so instead of practicing my organ lessons, I turned back to another favorite past time, writing. In five years, I wrote and published four children's books with a total of eighteen stories. One book for adults with eighty-one essays on the spiritual life and composed this autobiography. After the books were published, I resumed playing the organ, but it was a struggle to get back in the "swing." The study groups continued to meet each week as each of us grew into a deeper appreciation of our Catholic Faith.

Bob concentrated on his extensive stamp collection while he continued to teach for The Villages College which kept him mentally active. Engaging in a wild game of water volleyball three times a week and golfing with other residents weekly keeps him physically active while involvement in the Resident Advisory Council and FLICRA, Florida's Life Care Residents Association, keeps him politically active. I pray, read, write and teach while Bob runs from pillar to post accomplish-ing his agendas.

Living at Freedom Pointe in the Villages can be compared to living on a cruise ship with all the amenities, except this ship stays where it's anchored. Perhaps in the future, if we have to move into either the Assisted Living or Rehab sections of this retirement complex, we'll slow down, but don't count on that.

Chapter 26

FREEDOM POINTE MEANT FREEDOM
2009-20?? THE VILLAGES

Prior to coming to the Villages when we were 70, we had already decided to look into moving into an independent senior resident complex when we were about to turn 80. So when Freedom Pointe came along three years prior to that time, we immediately signed up to move in as soon as it was constructed. Since we didn't want to leave The Villages, this opportunity was just made for us.

We were very impressed by the Brookdale representatives and all the forthcoming plans. The marketing staff were a delight and everyone connected with the project was enthusiastic, joyful, and helpful. The buying experience couldn't have been better.

From the very beginning, the DINING experience was and is something we look forward to each day. The efficient dining room staff sees to our every need in a polite and pleasant way. The food is excellent and there is always something new and interesting to eat. The food is presented attractively and the buffets are incredible. The Chefs keep bringing on new and interesting entrees and pastries which pass the palate test. Meal charges for guests are reasonable and below the market value, but equally delicious and varied.

The PUB is an especially popular place with friendly and helpful bartenders and servers. You can order most any drink you desire and order a variety of meals from the breakfast, lunch/dinner menu. The PUB adds to the welcoming atmosphere of the reception area. As you walk into Freedom Pointe, you see residents and friends enjoying themselves as they sip a glass of wine or a favorite cocktail as they listen to musical entertainment or watch the latest sporting event.

The HOUSKEEPING staff members are pleasant and efficient. They come when assigned and do their work with a helpful attitude. We feel they really care about us and our condominiums. It's a pleasure to know that our homes are being honored by these young women and their desire to please.

The MAINTENANCE staff has exceeded all our expectations. The best part is the way they go about their work. We have never experienced such enthusiastic and caring men. Their joyful, loving and helpful attendance to their duties bring joy to each of us each day even when we see each other as we roam about the building. All the associates seem like a part of our large family.

There is a great range of RESIDENT PROGRAMS from which to choose. At this time we only participate in some of these choices because we still have much to do in our private lives. However, when we have the time we always enjoy the activities and the participants. The activities are bringing the community into a healthy lifestyle and creating friendships day by day. We have taken the leadership role in sponsoring two evening programs: classic movies of the 30's and 40's and professionally taped lecture series.

The MANAGERIAL STAFF did so much to make our transition to Freedom Pointe a delight. The ASSOCIATES are friendly, helpful and eager to please. They never made us feel that we or our questions or problems were a pain for them.

Each one pulled together to aid us in any difficulty. It was a very positive experience and we are always grateful for their warm and loving ways.

People ask us if we like Freedom Pointe and we always answer "NO," we "LOVE IT!" What's there not to like. A comfortable condo, a beautiful and safe building, great people, fantastic food, and plenty of fun things to do to keep us happy and well. Even the walk to the garage has become a positive experience. It's made us walk. Sometimes I enjoy walking the halls so much, I make excuses to go downstairs or out to the garage or porch. I hate to walk, but I love walking about in our new "mansion." We feel like millionaires and we're living a millionaire lifestyle..... at last.

Everyone is impressed with what they see. We always say: "This is the very best decision we ever made. Now, we are comfortable, secure and all our needs are well served."

Chapter 27

SURPRISE! YOU WON!

2013 THE VILLAGES, FL

"I did?!" said I, amazed.

"Yes! Your ice cream creation entitled HEAVENLY TRASH was selected by the Working Cow Ice Cream Company to be Freedom Pointe's Independent Living signature ice cream flavor. You, Joan, are now the 'Supreme Queen of Ice Cream at Freedom Pointe,'" the Dining Room Manager announced one happy day in the Fall.

What a thrill and what a surprise! When the contest was announced, I ran upstairs, found a small piece of paper and quickly wrote down the following recipe:

"French vanilla ice cream, crushed M & Ms, dried raisins, dried cranberries and chopped pecans."
I labeled this recipe: HEAVENLY TRASH

Grabbing my small piece of paper, I rushed downstairs to the studio and placed my signature ice cream creation idea into the proper slotted box. I figured I would be the first entry. It took less than a minute to come up with the idea. Like a flash, the idea popped into my brain. A couple of years later I learned that there had been at least 40 entries. Now I was really shocked!

A few months later, Working Cow invited a bus load of residents to come to St. Petersburg, FL to tour their plant and to taste this new ice cream flavor. The factory is quite small and their company ships orders only inside the state of Florida. They also supply their Working Cow Ice Cream shops in the state.

After the tour of the factory, tasting time for HEAVENLY TRASH had finally arrived. It was also a first for me, since I had never mixed the ingredients together to test the concoction in my own kitchen. The testing moment was at hand. The manager handed me a solidly frozen quart container of my ice cream and a small plastic spoon and the tasting began - well, almost.

The first challenge: how to remove the lid from the frozen carton?

The second challenge: using a flimsy plastic spoon, how could I scoop a large enough amount of frozen ice cream into my mouth in order to test the taste? Even before I had managed to put even a thin layer of Heavenly Trash into my mouth, my friends started asking "Is it good?" and "Do you like it?" and "Hurry, and share it with us!"

I assured them that "I will as soon as I could get enough of the frozen ice cream on the plastic spoon to tell anything!"

"Besides that, I can't discern the flavor because I have a cough drop in my mouth and that's all I can taste."

"I'm sorry, but I think we will have to wait until lunch to share it. By then, the ice cream will have become soft enough to eat."

Luckily, every spoonful of HEAVENLY TRASH did pass the taste test according to each one of the twenty tasters.

Eighteen months later our Independent Living complex agreed to share the signature ice cream with the other three buildings on the campus. Now, three years later, the Company has decided to market my concoction statewide in the Working Cow Ice Cream Parlors. It's delicious and very popular with all who have eaten it, like my friends, Al, John and others, who choose it for dessert every night instead of parfaits or pie, brownies or Crème Brulee, cookies or cake.

There's only one rub to this tale: If I had known that HEAVENLY TRASH was going to win; if I had been mercenary; if I had been wiser in the ways of the world; and if I had even asked what would happen IF, who knows what fortune might be mine "IF ONLY!" By the way, I did receive a beautiful silver, diamond, and pearl crown which I wear occasionally just for the fun of it and, of course, it isn't really real, but I do love it anyway.

Had I known my creation was going to be a winner and such a hit, I wish I'd been smart enough to sell the idea instead of just giving it away. But then, I never was much of a salesperson no matter what I tried to sell. No matter, it's been fun watching residents enjoy my creation. Maybe I'll make my fortune selling my six books.

P.S. Working Cow made one change to my recipe; no M&Ms, just small chunks of chocolate. When you make it yourself, try using crushed M&Ms. They make it colorful and add crunch along with the pecans. Enjoy!

Chapter 28

WHERE WE HUNG OUR HATS
HOMES ACQUIRED MOSTLY BY CHANCE
1952-2009

August 1952: Lake Forest, IL 122 N. Wildwood

I graduated from Lake Forest College and as our wedding day approached, one of Bob's fraternity brothers and his wife suggested we look into renting the space which they were about to vacate. So we looked it over and rented it; a three-room, attic apartment with sloping ceilings in a red, brick bungalow located in Lake Forest, Illinois near the college football field. We shared the first floor bath with the owners. We walked everywhere or rode the North Shore train.

June 1953: Evanston, IL 319 Dempster St.

After Bob's graduation we moved up in the world to a fourth floor walk-up, two-room apartment in a brown, brick apartment/hotel three blocks from Lake Michigan in Evanston, Illinois. Finally, we had our own bathroom, but slept on a Murphy bed which dropped down out of the closet into the kitchen. We shared our bedroom with a utility cabinet, kitchen sink, refrigerator, stove, small appliances, dining table & chairs and our clothes. Our first TV graced the living room with a pink velvet couch and teal blue fireside chairs from my parent's house.

June 1954: Medinah, IL 6N165 Circle Dr.

Next, I moved my pregnant self out to Medinah, Illinois. I lived in the country with my father on his 120-acre "estate" while Bob served with the occupation troops for eighteen months in Germany. Our daughter, Peggy, was born there. We enjoyed living with her Grandpa Joe and Uncle Don, who was stationed at Fort Sheridan. Being surrounded by a multitude of family made this a most pleasant interlude during those long months of separation.

August 1955: New London, WI 319 Wisconsin St.

When Bob returned home from Germany, we moved to New London, WI. and rented the first floor of an old two-story house. Our apartment consisted of a living room, two open bedrooms which we screened off by hanging drapes across the wide openings, a large kitchen, one bath and an unheated back room for hanging laundry when the weather proved too cold and snow covered the ground. A young couple, who fought daily and whose baby screamed and cried whenever the father was home, lived in the apartment above us. One day I discovered that they could look into our bedroom through the open floor vent located just above our bed and in the ceilings in all of our rooms. These vents allowed our heat to escape up into their apartment which meant we were cold and they were barely warm. After a year of that situation, we moved to a small, one-story house across town.

June 1956: New London, WI 209 West Quincy St.

This second house, near the church and the high school, proved to be quite pleasant. We entered the two-story house through the glassed-in-porch where Peggy could play safely and be warm in the winter. The living room was adjacent to the porch. The kitchen was old but adequate and the small room beside it served as our dining room and daytime nursery for Tom who was born in New London. Shoveling coal into the furnace every day caused the heat to fluctuate between too hot and too cold throughout the house. An enclosed, narrow staircase led to two small bedrooms on the second floor, which could have been a fire trap. The only bathroom was located on the first floor.

August 1957: Champaign, 501 South Westlawn

Our move to Champaign, Illinois found us renting a very nice ranch style home with two bedrooms, one bath, a nice kitchen, living room and a full basement which Bob used as a study. It was in excellent condition with a nice yard and a garden overgrown with wild asparagus behind a small patio. It's here where we first met "Mr. Roach." At night, when we flipped on the light switch large brown roaches scampered into the nooks and crannies to hide. We owned a Sears suds saving washing machine. To save water, the machine pumped the sudsy water into a garbage can. For the next load, I could suck the used water back into the machine. That was all well and good except, when I pumped too many tubs of sudsy water into the can, I ended up with excess sudsy water out all over the kitchen floor and elsewhere.

June 1958-1964: Urbana, IL 1302 Briarcliff Dr.

During the summer, we borrowed the down payment from my father and purchased a prefabricated National Home on a street loaded with young families. The five of us enjoyed tight relationships as we shared the small living room, kitchen/utility room, one bath and three small bedrooms. We ate in the kitchen lined up at a folding bar. The fenced back yard was large and treeless. An ugly soft maple tree dominated the front yard under which the neighborhood children gathered to play and to argue. After we hired an exterminator to explode an insecticide "bomb" into this cozy yellow house, we lived happily here roach free. We even repaid the loan back to my father in a couple of years. It was so nice to have a home of our own.

June 1964-1977: Urbana, IL: 301 West Pennsylvania Ave.

The next move came about because of a bridge game with a couple we knew from church. As we sat there playing bridge, I kept eyeing the charm of the two-story Boston Colonial House, which was for sale. By the end of the evening we made arrangements to return the next day to take a more serious look. We decided to purchase the house that day.

The first floor consisted of a large living room with a fire place, separate dining room, nice size kitchen, a large step-down family room across the back of the house. There were three bedrooms upstairs and another a full bath. The basement consisted of a playroom, laundry/work room and a coal bin, which was turned into a bedroom. The house felt like a mansion. The five of us soon lost contact with each other as each resident chose their own special space. Mine was the windowed room behind the living room fireplace along the driveway. Bob in the family room, Peggy in her bedroom, Tom in the coal bin bedroom, Jim in the living room and Peanut, the dog, on the deck.

We soon demolished the dilapidated single car garage and added a double garage with an automatic electric door powered by an exterior extension cord. When we sold this house, the realtor insisted that the cord needed to be replaced by official wiring. The house was located near the high school and the neighborhood park which sponsored programs and games in the summer and fall. The children literally lived at the park and eventually the high school. No carpooling was necessary, Bob walked to the University, the children were bused across town to the Catholic School and I traveled in the car to wherever my interests or needs led me.

January 1977-1981: St. Joseph, IL 145 West Woodland Drive

After the children left for college and were married, Bob and I yearned for a simpler lifestyle which led us to seek a home in a small town nearby. After extensive searching, we finally found a charming tan three bedroom brick ranch house on a quarter acre of land, ten miles east of Urbana in St. Joseph, Illinois. This move proved to be a lot more work than "falling into a just right house" on a whim, as happened the other times. Of course, we redecorated the interior, but pretty much left the yard alone with its majestic oak trees and an abundance of squirrels. Joan walked to work at the bank in town. Our years there were slow, simple and secluded.

July 1981-1986: Clemson, SC 110 Strode Circle

In June of 1981, we returned to life in the fast lane once again. Bob took a position as Dean of the College of Liberal Arts at Clemson University in Clemson, SC. A most suitable one-story ranch with a full basement fell into our path with a simple phone call from the owner. He'd read in the local paper that Bob had been hired so he called to offer us his house. It sounded ideal and over the phone we bought the house, sight unseen. Thank God, this house was perfect; no need for any changes. As soon as the van was unloaded, we served a dinner party for four new friends who had helped in the transition. Then we were off and running.

December 1986-1994: Clemson, SC 145 Folger St.

For this house see chapters: RETREATS SOMETIMES LEAD TO MORE THAN HOLINESS and TRANSFORMING OUR DREAM HOUSE. This house was sold before it went on the market.

June 1994-2000: Clemson, SC 105 Cardinal Dr.

When Bob retired and we planned to move out of town, a friend offered to rent us his mother's house until we decided on our plans. We jumped at the chance. Staying in town turned out to be the best option, so we bought this house and put time into redecorating. We also designed and landscaped the yard and garden area. Later, we dressed the dark brown brick ranch house with white vinyl windows and painted the doors and the trim. I loved how those windows looked, felt and operated. No more pitted aluminum to touch and no more swollen wooden windows to struggle to open.

June 2000-2009: The Villages, FL 1731 Palo Alto Ave

Off to Florida after the spontaneous over the phone purchase of a white stucco one-story house on the eighth fairway of Terra del Sol golf course in The Villages. This time we went from a relatively quiet life of retirement in a small college town to a bustling recreational retirement community with activities galore. We joined everything imaginable. A minimum of redecorating was needed, but major landscaping was absolutely required. Life under the palm trees and the constant Florida sun proved delightful, but we did miss the lake activities which were soon replaced by golf.

December 2009-: The Villages, FL 1550 El Camino Real #236

As our 79th birthdays grew near, we prudently chose to prepare for the future. We bought a two bedroom/two bath condo in the newly opened Freedom Point Independent Living seven-story condominium along with lots of amenities and activities and we're still in The Villages, praise God. It's like living on a landlocked cruise ship. It is also part of a continuing care operation which includes assisted living, memory care and rehabilitation facilities available when and if needed. What a wonderful way to end the responsibility of home ownership. Our last stop: Highland Memorial Park Cemetery in Ocala, FL. sleeping head to head in a mausoleum. No more redecorating, remodeling, landscape work or moving, except, perhaps, being transferred from Purgatory to Heaven after we've been cleaned up and made ready to meet the "BOSS."

Chapter 29

MY LIFE AT A GLANCE

RIVER FOREST, IL

October 7, 1930 born at Oak Park Hospital, Oak Park, IL; lived at 1427 Park Ave, River Forest, IL; Father Dr. Joseph C. Sodaro, Mother Margret R. McIntosh Sodaro; Siblings: Dean 1928, Don 1933, Janet 1936, Peggy 1940.

September 1935 attended Willard Grade School Ashland Avenue, River Forest, IL, K-5; St. Vincent Ferrer Catholic Grade School on Lathrop Avenue, grades 6 & 7, Roosevelt Grade School on Lathrop Avenue, grade 8.

September 1944-June 1948 attended Oak Park River Forest High School.

ST MARYS OF THE WOODS, IN

September 1948-December 1950 studied at St Mary of the Woods College near Terre Haute, IN

LAKE FOREST, IL

January 1950-June 1952 transferred to Lake Forest College, Lake Forest, IL and graduated in June 1952.

MEDINAH, IL

June 1952 stayed in Medinah, IL during the summer to help my Mother prepare for our wedding on August 16th.

LAKE FOREST, IL

August 1952 married Bob on August 16th and moved to our first apartment at 122 Wildwood Lane, Lake Forest, IL. It was a three-room attic apartment in a brick bungalow just one block from the College football field. We shared the house with the owners and shared their bathroom on the 1st floor.

September 1952-June 1953 taught 3rd grade at Lake Bluff Grade School in Lake Bluff, IL and Bob worked on his BA degree.

EVANSTON, IL

June 1953 Bob graduated from LFC and in the Fall he began graduate school at Northwestern University in Evanston, IL. We moved to 319 Dempster Street Evanston, IL (a 4 story apartment hotel near Lake Michigan). During the summer, I worked as a waitress at a diner and tutored a 4th grade student in reading. In the Fall, I began teaching first and second grades at East Prairie School in Skokie, IL.

November 1953 Bob was drafted into the army and temporarily suspended work toward his graduate degrees in American History. He was stationed at Fort Leonard Wood in Missouri for 16 weeks of basic training.

November 1953 My Mother died of cancer. She is buried in Queen of Heaven Cemetery Hinsdale, IL.

January 1954 Bob was sent to Germany for an 18-month tour of duty with the occupation troops.

MEDINAH, IL 6N165 Circle Drive

January 1954 moved home to stay with my Father at 6N165 Circle Drive, Medinah, IL. I was pregnant with Peggy, but continued to teach in Skokie, IL until June.

November 1954 Peggy was born at Oak Park Hospital with her Grandfather assisting. We remained in Medinah until Bob returned from Europe.

While there, my Father married Lucille Berliner, so my family acquired not only a Step-Mother, but also four additional sisters and their families. Our Family now included nine grown children plus the in-laws and a houseful of grandchildren. It was fun.

NEW LONDON, WI

August 1955 Bob returned to the United States and we moved to 319 Wisconsin Avenue and later to 209 West Quincy Street, New London, WI. Bob taught American History at New London High School and coached debate.

March 1957 Tom was born at New London Hospital.

CHAMPAIGN/ URBANA, IL

August 1957 moved to 501 South Westlawn Street, Champaign, IL so Bob could begin again on his graduate studies towards a PhD in American History.

I worked part time in a day care center; worked as a file clerk for CS Johnson Construction Co. at their batching plant.

June 1958 bought our first home at 1302 Briarcliff Drive, Urbana, IL. It was a prefab National Home. I took in ironing, kept the neighbor's children and on Saturdays I taught Catechism.

November 1959 Jim was born at Burnham Hospital in Champaign, IL.

The children attended Kindergarten at Wiley School in Urbana, IL; St. Mary's and Holy Cross Catholic Grade Schools in Champaign, IL; and Urbana Jr. and Sr. High Schools in Urbana, IL

Eventually, I became more immersed in ministry work at St. Patrick's Parish and in Urbana civic affairs: President of Alpha Phi Alumnae 1958-1960; President of St. Patrick's Altar and Rosary Society 1962-1964; Parish Council member 1971-73.

May 1966-January 1977 moved to 301 West Pennsylvania Avenue, Urbana, IL; taught kindergarten briefly at Hays School, Urbana, IL in the Fall of 1966; helped establish a Birthright chapter in Champaign/Urbana and a Montessori School; served as a teacher's aide and did some data processing for a U of I study in reading; helped establish and worked full time at The Good Shepherd House of Prayer in Urbana 1974-1976; later worked as a teller at the Bank of Illinois in Champaign.

Bob taught Social Studies at Urbana High School and served as a member of the Urbana School Board. He also finished his graduate degrees in 1958 & 1963. In 1967 he was appointed as Associate Dean of the College of Liberal Arts and Sciences at the University of Illinois and was tenured.

The Children: Peggy studied at Lawrence University and Columbia University 1972-1986 and married June 2, 1979; Tom studied at Illinois State University at Normal, IL 1975-1979 and married June 26,1976; Jim attended Eastern Illinois University from 1978-1979 and married June 7, 1980.

ST JOSEPH, IL

January 1977-June 1981 moved to 18 West Woodland Drive, St Joseph, IL. Bob was on sabbatical leave and the children were in college.

I worked at the Bank of St. Joseph as a teller/bookkeeper until September 1978. Made 25 Liturgical Banners for St. Patrick's Church. Searched for rare books to be repaired and cleaned at the University of Illinois Library in 1980.

CLEMSON, SC

June 1981 moved to 110 Strode Circle, Clemson, SC. Bob was appointed Dean of the College of Liberal Arts at Clemson University.

I became involved with St. Andrew's Parish and enjoyed working with Bob as he served as Dean.

October 20, 1983 my father died in California. He was buried in Queen of Heaven Cemetery next to my mother.

I started a group to study the writings of Luisa Piccarreta which concerns Living in The Divine Will; I served as a leader of the Charismatic Prayer Group and became completely involved with parish activities for our entire stay in Clemson.

January 1986 moved to 145 Folger Street on Lake Hartwell in Clemson, SC and did major renovation of the house and grounds.

May 1991 my brother, Dean died of lung cancer.

July 1994 moved to 105 Cardinal Drive, Clemson S.C. which we refurbished inside and did major landscaping to the yard and gardens.

July 1996-June 2000 when Bob retired, he became Dean Emeritus and Professor Emeritus and continued to serve Clemson University as a consultant to the Faculty Manual.

I continued my study group on the Divine Will, served as a spiritual director, a Eucharistic Minister at Mass and to the sick and a Lector.

THE VILLAGES, FL

June 2000-December 2009 retired to Florida and moved into 1731 Palo Alto Avenue on the 8th Fairway of the Palo Alto golf course.

After redecorating yet another home, a whirlwind of activities commenced as we became involved in teaching and church ministry, golf and exercise, games and clubs, music and dance lessons, stamp collecting and writing, cultural activities and countless social activities.

November 2009-20?? moved into an Independent Living Condominium called Freedom Pointe, at 1550 El Camino Real #236, The Villages, Fl.

Bob continued to teach history for The Villages College until April 2015. I have enjoyed writing and publishing four books for children (18 stories) and two books for adults. My study group on Living in the Divine Will continues and has expanded the choices of subjects.

It has been a full and rewarding life.

Printed in the United States
By Bookmasters